The
ARDENNES BATTLEFIELDS
DECEMBER 1944 – JANUARY 1945

Previous Page: *The face of battle. Sgt Joseph Holmes of Coy C, 320th Inf Regt, 35th Inf Div, seen on January 10.*

This Page: *Snowsuited soldiers in the ruins of St. Vith. They are from Coy C, 48th AIB, 7th Armd Div, January 24.*

The
ARDENNES
BATTLEFIELDS
DECEMBER 1944 – JANUARY 1945

Leo Marriott & Simon Forty

Published in the United States of America and Great Britain in 2017 by
CASEMATE PUBLISHERS
1950 Lawrence Road, Havertown, PA 19083
and
The Old Music Hall, 106-108 Cowley Road, Oxford, OX4 1JE

Copyright 2017 © Simon Forty

ISBN-13: 978-1-61200-534-8

Produced by Greene Media Ltd., 34 Dean Street, Brighton BN1 3EG

Cataloging-in-publication data is available from the Library of Congress and the British Library.

The information in this book is true and complete to the best of our knowledge. All recommendations are made without any guarantee on the part of the Authors or Publisher, who also disclaim any liability incurred in connection with the use of this data or specific details.

All Internet site information provided was correct when received from the Authors. The Publisher can accept no responsibility for this information becoming incorrect.

10 9 8 7 6 5 4 3 2 1

Printed and bound in China

For a complete list of Casemate titles please contact:

CASEMATE PUBLISHERS (US)
Telephone (610) 853-9131, Fax (610) 853-9146
E-mail:
casemate@casematepublishers.com

CASEMATE PUBLISHERS (UK)
Telephone (01865) 241249, Fax (01865) 794449
E-mail:
casemate-uk@casematepublishers.co.uk

Below: *6th Armd Div halftrack near Foy.*

Note

1. All dates, unless specified, are between June 1944 and February 1945.

2 There are at least three languages involved in place names and names of geographical features in the Ardennes: Belgian, Luxembourgish, and German. So Clerf is the German for Clervaux (Belgian/French) or Klierf (Lux); the River Clerf (Eng) or Clerve (FR), is also the Klerf (German) or Klierf (Lux). And to complicate matters, after Clervaux the Clerve is called the Woltz. The River Roer (FR and Dutch) is Rur in German. I have tried to use the names the Allies used.

CONTENTS

INTRODUCTION

ARDENNES –16 DEC 1944 – 25 JAN 1945
RHINELAND –5 MAR 1945 – 21 MAR 1945

EIGHTH AIR FORCE   NINTH AIR FORCE   IX TROOP CARRIER COMMAND   RAF BOMBER COMMAND

MILES   0   5   10   15
KILOMETRES   0   5   10   15   20

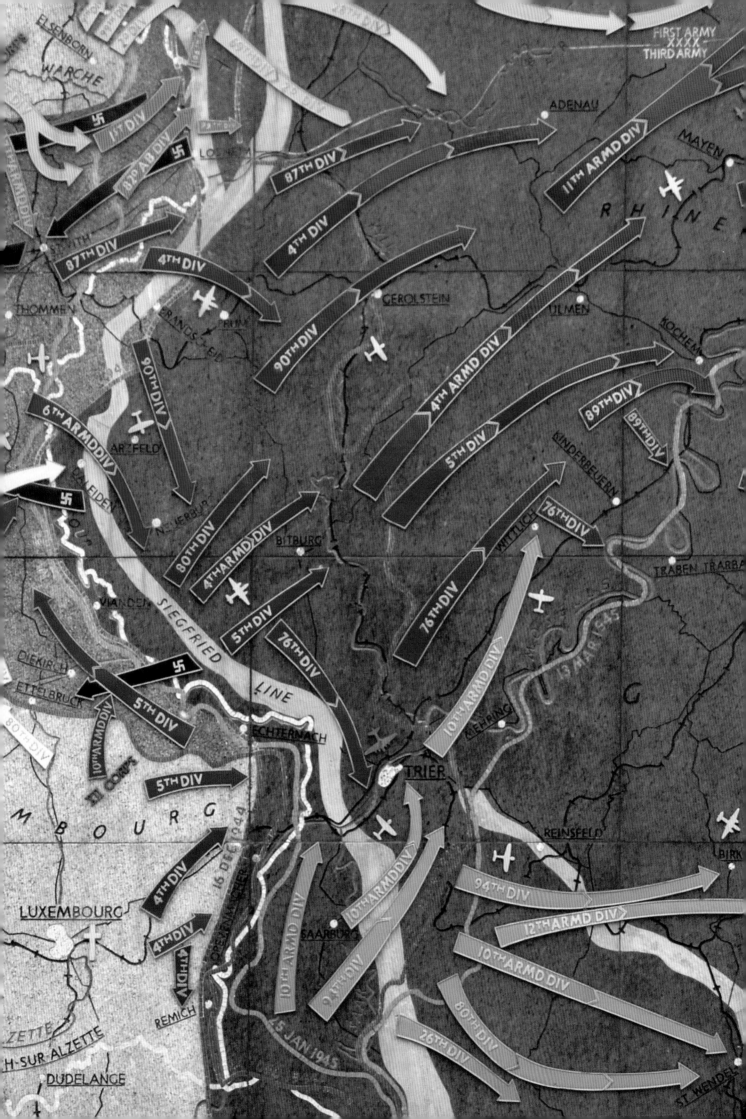

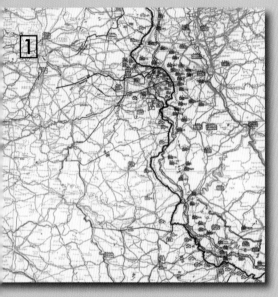

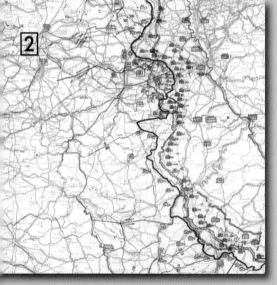

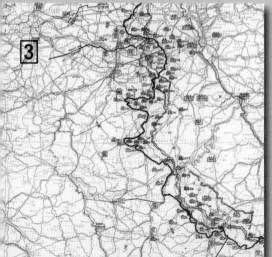

To the north of Third Army, within the First Army sector, lay the Ardennes Front. In December 1944 it was popularly known as the "Ghost Front," a cold quiet place where the artillery of both sides fired only when they wanted to register possible future targets and where patrols probed enemy lines more to keep in practice than for any aggressive reason. German watched American and American watched German within small-arms range of one another.

For over two months now each side had strenuously avoided irritating the other along the whole of the 85-mile front. It was here that Adolf Hitler, chose to stage his final all-out gamble designed to smash the Western Allies and drive them back to the sea. *Unternehmen Wacht am Rhein* (Operation Watch on the Rhine) was undoubtedly one of the best-kept secrets of the war. Three armies—the Sixth SS-Panzer under SS-Oberst-Gruppenführer Joseph "Sepp" Dietrich, the Fifth Panzer under General der Panzertruppe Baron Hasso von Manteuffel, and the largely infantry Seventh Armee, commanded by General der Panzertruppe Erich Brandenberger, were secretly assembled into *Heeresgruppe* (Army Group) B under Generalfeldmarschall Walter Model.

The plan was to break through on the Ardennes front between Monschau in the north, and Echternach in the south. The attack would brush aside the weakly held American positions, aim to cross the Meuse between Liège and Namur, bypass Brussels, and reach Antwerp within the week. The Western Allies would never recover from such an onslaught and would have to sue for a separate peace. That was the risky plan, which the Führer himself had devised. And along roads and tracks spread with straw to muffle the noise, over 250,000 troops, nearly 2,000 pieces of artillery, and 1,000 tanks and assault guns, moved slowly and quietly into their attack positions. H-hour was to be at first light on December 16, 1944. In addition to the frontal attack, picked men, masquerading as Americans, in U.S. army uniforms and vehicles, were to be employed to get behind the front lines, seize vital points such as the bridges over the Meuse, spread rumors, give false orders, and create panic and confusion.

The result was the largest battle the U.S. Army has ever fought.

TIMELINE

September 16 Führer conference at which Ardennes offensive first mentioned.

September 25 Führer conference at which the idea for *Wacht am Rhein* is further expounded. Various names are associated with the offensive: *Wacht am Rhein* (Guard on the Rhine) is from a popular song; *Herbstnebel* (Autumn mist) was used later. "*Christrose*" is also used, usually linked to XLVII Panzerkorps.

October 22 Hitler outlines the offensive to key advisers and Siegfried Westphal and Hans Krebs, chiefs of staff of von Rundstedt (OB West) and Model (Heeresgruppe B).

End November–mid-December German build-up in concentration area. Mock radio traffic and tight radio security in area.

November 25 Original target date for launch of offensive.

December 1 German recon activity along Ardennes Front forbidden from this date onwards.

First week of December Korps commanders informed.

December 7 Maastricht meeting sees Eisenhower, Bradley, and Montgomery agree on New Year offensives.

December 10 Divisional commanders informed. Hitler leaves Berlin by train to establish HQ at the *Adlerhorst* (Eagle's eyrie) in Bad Nauheim.

December 12 Attack divisions begin deployment under strict security.

December 13 Americans begin attack on Roer dams.

December 15–16 German troops given detailed orders.

December 16 X-Day (aka *Tag Null*) *Wacht am Rhein* launched.

December 17 Situation at last light:
Sixth SS-Panzerarmee has made small gains, but is now stopped in area Monschau–Elsenborn by determined U.S. resistance.
Fifth Panzerarmee advancing slowly towards St. Vith, but faster to the south.
Seventh Armee across River Clerve but making slow progress.
U.S. troops from Third and Ninth Armies begin deployment to reinforce First Army.
SHAEF releases 82nd and 101st AB Divs to 12th Army Group and they are despatched to Ardennes front.

December 18 Target date for Meuse bridgeheads to have been taken.
Fifth Panzerarmee's XLVII Panzerkorps has made a sizeable breach in the U.S. front, inflicting heavy casualties on some units (eg, 110th Inf Regt).
Situation at last light: Sixth SS-Panzerarmee still making slow progress, but attack by KG Peiper halted and isolated.
Fifth Panzerarmee making progress around flanks of St. Vith and has isolated some 8,000 U.S. troops in the Schnee Eifel.
XLVII Panzerkorps reaches outer defenses of Bastogne, but main mission of army to push on to the Meuse remains in force.
Seventh Armee reaches Wiltz.
British XXX Corps ordered to get troops down to the Meuse to protect the vulnerable bridges as soon as possible.

December 19 Allied conference at Verdun—Patton proposes to turn U.S. Third Army northwards and attack with three divisions on the 22nd: all agree.
All three German armies continue to advance, although some units, eg 12th SS-Panzer Div, have been without fuel for twelve hours. On their flanks U.S. First and Third Armies regroup.

December 20 Because of Sixth SS-Panzerarmee's lack of progress, von Rundstedt orders shift of main point of effort to Fifth Panzerarmee which is still progressing towards the Meuse, sweeping past Bastogne, which is now all but isolated.
Seventh Armee advances along Bastogne–Arlon road and finally seizes Diekirch.
HQ 21st Army Group (Montgomery) takes command of U.S. First and Ninth Armies from 12th Army Group (Bradley) and First Army launches limited counterattack towards St. Vith.

Below: *The German advance reached its farthest point in this period—* **4** *December 25;* **5** *27; and* **6** *29.*

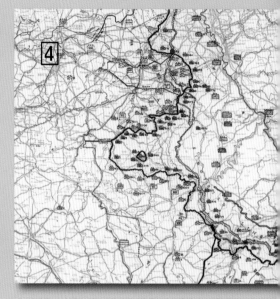

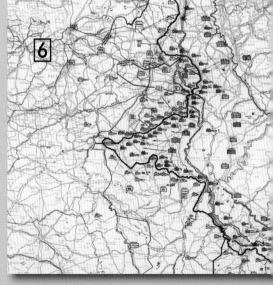

Below: *The Allied advances began to erode the German salient in this period, December 31–January 8.*
1 *December 31;* **2** *January 4; and* **3** *January 8.*

December 21 Sixth SS-Panzerarmee still cannot relieve Kampfgruppe Peiper.
Fifth Panzerarmee finally takes St. Vith.
Bastogne now completely encircled but McAuliffe of 101st AB Div, replies "Nuts" to Germans' call to surrender.
Heeresgruppe B brings up 9th Panzer and 15th PzGr Divs as reinforcements.
Seventh Armee's leading elements reach Libramont. The weather has now turned freezing cold.

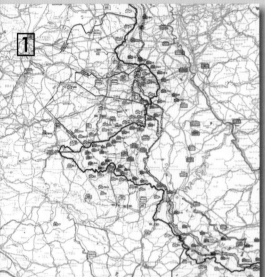

December 23 First clear day, so 3,000+ Allied aircraft fly missions in German combat and rear areas, also supply besieged Bastogne.
Fifth Panzerarmee now five miles from Dinant and the Meuse, but is halted by BR 29th Armd Bde, U.S. 2nd Armd Div, and fuel shortage.
Seventh Armee under attack from U.S. Third Army but manages to hold line of the River Sauer.

December 24 Offensive has pushed as far west as it will get.
Sixth SS-Panzerarmee now on defensive along line Monschau–Elsenborn–Stavelot–Grandmenil.
Remnants of KG Peiper manage to break out.
Fifth Panzerarmee now in Conneux–Celles area.
Spearhead of 2nd Pz Div is attacked by fighter-bombers.
Fifth Panzerarmee unable to mount concentrated attack because of its threatened flank.
Elements of British XXX Corps now in positions on Meuse between Givet and Liège.

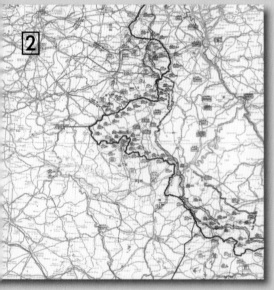

December 25 German offensive has ground to a halt from lack of fuel, ammunition, and supplies, while everywhere U.S. counterattacks are making progress. Good flying weather persists. Spearhead of 2nd Pz Div surrounded and destroyed by U.S. 2nd Armd Div.

December 26 First *Wacht am Rhein*-related message sent using Enigma machine.
Siege of Bastogne broken by arrival of lead tanks of U.S. Third Army's 4th Armd Div.
Good flying weather continues and all three German armies suffer major losses from air and ground attack.
Hitler refuses to rescind order that Bastogne be taken at all costs.

December 27 British XXX Corps and U.S. 2nd Armd Div halt German advance in the Celles sector.
Pressure from U.S. First and Third Armies is increasing.
Allied High Command propose deep penetration to pinch off the entire German salient. It is clear that the Germans have lost the initiative as more and more of their formations are being forced onto the defensive.

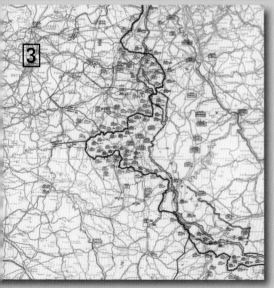

December 28 Eisenhower and Montgomery meet at Hasselt, Belgium.
U.S. Third Army prepares for counteroffensive between Rivers Sauer and Wiltz.
Conference at Hitler's HQ to discuss Operation *Nordwind* in Alsace.

December 30 U.S. Third Army begins to advance on Houffalize.

1945
January 1 Luftwaffe launches Operation *Bodenplatte*.
U.S. III Corps counterattacks around Bastogne with limited success, while VIII Corps attacks SW face of German salient with considerable success.

Germans launch Operation *Nordwind*—a two-pronged attack by Heeresgruppe G in Alsace and towards Strasbourg.

January 2 U.S. Third Army continues advance, taking Gérimont, Mande St.-Étienne, and Senonchamps.
Fifth Panzerarmee asks for permission to withdraw but Hitler refuses.
German pressure in U.S. Seventh Army's sector (*Nordwind*) continues and is especially critical in VI Corps' area.

January 3 U.S. First Army mounts offensive towards Houffalize further to reduce enemy salient and link up with Third Army.
German *Nordwind* forces expand their salient towards Bitche.
French ordered to garrison Strasbourg, releasing U.S. troops for operations further north against *Nordwind*.

January 4 Heavy snow prevents Allied attack on German northern flank in Ardennes, but Fifth Panzerarmee is being slowly pushed back and German attacks on Bastogne come to a halt.
Hitler agrees to Sixth SS-Panzerarmee's withdrawal from Eifel area. They are then sent to the Eastern Front where a massive Russian assault is anticipated.

January 5–8 Allies launch new assault between Stavelot and Marche.

January 6 Units of U.S. First and Third Armies still pressing forward.
Withdrawal of Sixth SS-Panzerarmee makes German position even more vulnerable, but Hitler refuses to withdraw east of the Rhine.
In the south, U.S. Seventh Army still attempting to reduce Bitche salient.

January 7–12 Fifth Panzerarmee and Sixth SS-Panzerarmee carry out major withdrawal, while Seventh Armee endeavors, unsuccessfully, to hold southern flank.
New German offensive in Strasbourg area on January 7 and pressure continues against French First and U.S. Seventh armies.

January 13 U.S. attacks continue all along Ardennes Front, while British XXX Corps completes its task when 51st Highland Division reaches River Ourthe south of La Roche.
In southern sector French troops hold off repeated German attacks around Strasbourg.

January 16 British Second Army launches Operation Blackcock to eliminate German salient between the Meuse and the Roer (the Roermond Triangle).
Link-up between leading troops of the U.S. First Army (VII Corps) and U.S. Third Army (VIII Corps) near Houffalize.
German salient has now been reduced to half its former size.
In the south, U.S. 12th Armd Div of VI Corps, Seventh Army, opens an offensive against the Gambsheim bridgehead.

January 23 St. Vith retaken—virtually the end of the Bulge.

January 26 End of *Nordwind* offensive.

February 2 German forces are back at the original starting points along the Siegfried Line from which they launched their attack.

Below: *Between January 13 and 29 the front lines returned to their pre-bulge boundaries. Within weeks the Third Reich would implode.* **4** *January 13;* **5** *January 21; and* **6** *January 29.*

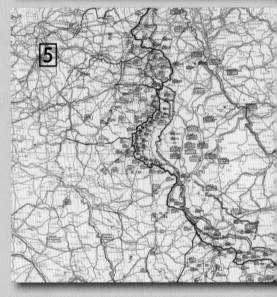

ALLIED ORDER OF BATTLE (abbreviated)

12th U.S. Army Group (Lt Gen Omar N. Bradley)

First U.S. Army (Lt Gen Courtney H. Hodges)
V Corps (Maj Gen Leonard T. Gerow)
  1st, 2nd, 9th,78th, and 99th Infantry divisions

VII Corps (Maj Gen Joseph Lawton Collins)
  2nd and 3rd Armored divisions
  83rd and 84th Infantry divisions

XVIII Airborne Corps (Maj Gen Matthew B. Ridgway)
  7th Armored Division
  30th and 75th Infantry divisions
  82nd Airborne Division (from SHAEF Reserve
  December 17)

Third U.S. Army (Lt Gen George S. Patton, Jr.)
III Corps (Maj Gen John Millikin)
  4th and 6th Armored divisions
  26th, 35th, and 90th Infantry divisions

VIII Corps (Maj Gen Troy H. Middleton)
  9th and 11th Armored Divisions
  28th, 87th, and 106th Infantry divisions (survivors of

  106th to V Corps on December 20)
  17th (from XVIII Corps on January 1) and 101st
  (from SHAEF Reserve December 17) Airborne
  divisions

XII Corps (Maj Gen Manton S. Eddy)
  4th, 5th, 80th Infantry divisions
  10th Armored Division

Ninth U.S. Army (Lt Gen William H. Simpson)
  5th and 7th Armd and 30th Inf divisions (to First
  Army)

XIII Corps (Maj Gen Alvan C. Gillem)
  102nd Infantry Division

XVI Corps (Maj Gen J. B. Anderson) Not operational

XIX Corps (Maj Gen Raymond S. McLain)
  8th, 29th, and 104th Infantry divisions

21st BR Army Group (FM Sir Bernard L. Montgomery)

XXX Corps (Lt Gen Sir Brian G. Horrocks)
  6th Airborne Division
  51st (Highland) and 53rd (Welsh) Infantry divisions
  29th and 33rd Armoured and 34th Army Tank Bdes

Corps Reserve
Guards Armoured Division
43rd (Wessex) Infantry Division

GERMAN ORDER OF BATTLE (abbreviated)

OB-West (Commander-in-Chief, West) (von Rundstedt) Heeresgruppe B (Model)

Fifth Panzerarmee (Gen Hasso von Manteuffel)
XLVII Panzerkorps (Gen Heinrich von Lüttwitz)
  2nd and 9th Panzer and Panzer Lehr divisions
  26th Volksgrenadier Division
  Führer Begleit Brigade (from reserve)

LXVI Armeekorps (Gen Walther Lucht)
  18th (+) and 62nd (-) Volksgrenadier divisions

LVIII Panzerkorps (Gen Walter Krüger)
  116th Panzer Division (-)
  560th Volksgrenadier Division (-)

XXXIX Armeekorps (Gen Karl Decker)
  167th Volksgrenadier Division

Sixth SS-Panzerarmee (SS-Oberstgruppenführer
"Sepp" Dietrich)
I SS-Panzerkorps (SS-Gruppenführer Hermann Priess)
  1st SS-Panzer Division (*Leibstandarte Adolf Hitler*)
  12th SS-Panzer Division (*Hitlerjugend*)
  150 Panzer Brigade
  3rd Fallschirmjäger Division
  12th and 277th Volksgrenadier divisions

II SS-Panzerkorps (General Wilhelm Bittrich)
  2nd (*Das Reich*) and 9th (*Hohenstaufen*) SS-Panzer
  divisions

LXVII Armeekorps (Gen Otto Hitzfeld)
  3rd Panzergrenadier Division
  246th, 272nd, and 326th Volksgrenadier divisions

Seventh Armee (Gen Erich Brandenberger)
LIII Armeekorps (von Rothkirch)
  9th Volksgrenadier Division
  15th Panzergrenadier Division
  79th Volksgrenadier Division and Führer Grenadier
  Brigade from reserve on December 22)

LXXX Armeekorps (General Franz Beyer)
  212th, 276th, and 340th Volksgrenadier divisions

LXXXV Armeekorps (General Baptist Kniess)
  5th FJR Division
  352nd Volksgrenadier Divisions

Reserves
  9th, 79th, and 167th Volksgrenadier divisions
  11th Panzer Division; Führer Grenadier and
  Führer Begleit brigades

U.S. First Army

From D-Day on, initially with Lt Gen Omar N. Bradley commanding, First Army made the hard yards through France, fighting off the beaches, slogging their way through the constriction of the bocage hedgerows to Saint-Lô, and creating the breakout through Operation Cobra. Having done that—and allowing Third Army and Patton to enjoy the publicity and Press plaudits for the speed of their advance through the weakly defended hinterland— First Army squeezed the retreating Germans into the Falaise Pocket.

Between the end of the Falaise Gap battles around August 21–22 and the opening German bombardment of December 16 that announced their offensive, First Army—now under Hodges—advanced impressively. The first Americans to enter Paris, they were also the first to cross the Siegfried Line into Germany in September 1944.

Next came the bloody battle of the Hürtgen Forest from September 19 to December 16—the longest single battle the U.S. Army has ever fought— and a high casualty figure: 33,000 killed and wounded (including non-combat casualties). During this time, farther north, First Army captured the first major German city taken by the Allies, Aachen, in another bloody battle fought October 2–21. During the fighting two of Hodges' best infantry divisions suffered heavy casualties, the 30th "Old Hickory" had roughly 3,000 men killed and wounded, while the Big Red One took at least 1,350 casualties (150 killed and 1,200 wounded).

On the day that the German offensive began, First Army's front ran from the Monschau Forest, south of Aachen and the Hürtgen Forest, to Echternach, some 75 miles south. In the north, V Corps' 2nd Inf Div was the most northerly unit. It had been pulled from the Schnee Eifel area to take part in an offensive against the Roer and Urft dams. They had just taken the village of Wahlerscheid and were out on a limb on December 16.

The next unit was 99th Inf Div, again part of V Corps. Recently arrived from England, the Checkerboard Division had no combat experience.

VIII Corps comprised 14th Cavalry Group—spread thinly over 9,000 yards with a troubling two-mile gap between the cavalry and the 99th— then the 106th Inf Div on the Schnee Eifel. They were complete greenhorns and their first action was to end tragically. To their right, 28th Inf Div was stretched over some 25 miles, recovering from 6,000 casualties in the battle of the Hürtgen Forest.

The final VIII Corps unit was battle-weary 4th Inf Div, also recovering from the Hürtgen and still 2,000 men understrength. Most of their 35-mile front was along the Sauer and Moselle rivers.

VIII Corps' mobile reserve was 9th Armd Div, also untested in action. Its CCA was in the front line; CCR was in reserve; CCB had been ordered north to the Roer Dams assault.

General Hodges
(1887–1966)

General Courtney Hicks Hodges came up the hard way. Flunking West Point (lack of ability in math was cited) he enlisted as a private soldier in 1906, and gaining a commission from the ranks in 1909, ending up only a year behind his fellow West Pointers. He fought with Pershing against Villa, won a Silver Star for gallantry and a Distinguished Service Cross for extraordinary heroism in action while serving with 6th Infantry Regiment, 5th Division, AEF. He would also gain three Army Distinguished Service Medals. He met and impressed Bradley while both were teaching at West Point, and their friendship flourished. This would prove helpful when Hodges took over Bradley's First Army, although Bradley fretted that his friend was more worrier than warrior (as Chet Hansen put it).

Left: *First Army units outside Eupen. An important nodal point just south of Aachen on the road to Malmédy, it was into this area that the abortive Operation Stösser launched an ad hoc German parachute unit. The plan was that it would be able to help open the road to Eupen for the advancing LXVII Armeekorps. It wouldn't have been able to do much even if the occasion had arisen, as Oberst von der Heydte's 870 men were so badly scattered that he was able to collect only 150 of them.*

Lt Gen Patton
(1885 –1945)

Since his untimely death caused by injuries sustained in a car wreck, myths have grown up around the short career of Lt Gen George Smith Patton, Jr. Hollywood, and a barnstorming performance by George C. Scott helped by seventy-five years of hindsight, have elevated the charismatic general to the pantheon of America's greatest warriors. The reality, as is usually the case, is more ambiguous. Associated with tanks and mobile warfare from early on—he was the only high-ranking Allied commander who had commanded tanks at brigade level in WWI—he had an adroit touch when handling armored warfare, as was made plain the moment his Third Army was pushed through the gap created by Operation Cobra. The Germans, who until then had not—as so many accounts propose—paid particular attention to him, were forced quickly to take note. Patton courted publicity, but his reputation during the war was double-edged as was shown by the furore surrounding the post-Sicily slapping incidents or his Knutsford speech in 1944. In the end, however, he repaid the faith his friend Eisenhower showed in him. He and his army were instrumental in ensuring the faltering German offensive was negated in the south.

U.S. Third Army

His army operational from August 1, Patton had taken advantage of the opportunity Operation Cobra afforded, and Third Army had broken out faster and farther than could possibly have been anticipated. Creating the lower pincer that closed the Falaise Pocket, Third Army quickly crossed the Seine and advanced on toward Lorraine. It was here, short of fuel, with extended supply lines, and in an unusually rainy fall that Third Army faltered. Metz proved a difficult stronghold that held out for a month, and "to capture the province of Lorraine, a problem which involved an advance of only 40 to 60 air miles, Third Army required over 3 months and suffered 50,000 casualties [6,657 killed, 36,406 wounded, 12,119 missing], approximately one-third of the total number of casualties it sustained in the entire European war." (Dr. Christopher Gabel.)

Finally, Metz fell and Third Army was able to launch an offensive towards the Westwall. In fact, the attack across the Saar River was already underway as the Germans opened the Ardennes Offensive. This forced Patton to scale down operations on the Saar, leaving it to his XX Corps, and for U.S. Seventh Army to take on some of Third Army's responsibilities (to whom Patton detached 87th Inf Div). In turn, this would stretch Seventh when it was attacked by Operation *Nordwind* in January 1945.

Patton wheeled Third Army toward the German attack and pushed on quickly to Bastogne, the key transport node in southern Belgium. On the 20th Patton moved the tactical echelon of Lucky Forward—the codename of his HQ—to Luxembourg City, to be closer to the action. Within a week of the attack, his III Corps was poised to relieve beleaguered Bastogne.

Patton was able to move his army with such speed and dexterity because he had assembled an excellent staff, although he had recently had to replace his Chief of Staff, Hugh Gaffey, whom he had moved to command 4th Armd Div replacing "Tiger Jack" Wood. It was 4th Armd Div that would break the encirclement of Bastogne when elements of Lt Col Creighton W. Abrams' 37th Tank Battalion broke through at Assenois.

Patton had also listened to Oscar Koch—"the best damned intelligence officer in any U.S. Army command"—who had identified the buildup of German troops in the Ardennes. The rest is history.

Above: *A party of VIPs at Julich. L–R: Maj Gen McLain (U.S. XIX Corps), FM Montgomery (British 21st Army Group), Winston Churchill (British Prime Minister), Maj Gen Gillem (U.S. XIII Corps) FM Brooke (British Chief Imperial Gen Staff), and Lt Gen Simpson (U.S. Ninth Army).*

Lt Gen Simpson
(1888–1980)

U.S. Ninth Army

Lt Gen William Simpson's army did not take part in the Battle of the Bulge, but many of its units did, passed over to First Army's control. On December 7 at Maastricht Eisenhower had agreed that Montgomery's 21st Army Group should attack across the Rhine in early January, and that Ninth Army should take part—but then came the bolt from the blue, and all eyes turned to the Ardennes. The most obvious and immediate assistance provided to First Army was in the form of 7th Armd Div. Resting around Maastricht following hard fighting at Overloon and on the banks of the Roer, 7th Armd Div hastened south (see pp. 100–103). Traffic jams and bad weather meant that they were unable to help stop the rout of the 106th Infantry Division, but the "Lucky Seventh" were to cover themselves in glory, defending St. Vith and disrupting the German timetable.

On December 16 and 17, Simpson proffered more support: 30th Inf Div —"Roosevelt's SS,"who had gained a reputation as one of the top infantry divisions in the ETO. The division moved south to the Malmédy–Stavelot area and were instrumental in the battles to cut off KG Peiper (see pp. 74–75 and 88–89). Attacked from both sides, Peiper from the Trois-Ponts direction and Knittel from the other bank, 30th Division held firm and forced Peiper, his spearhead cut off from fuel and other supplies, to abandon his heavy equipment and leave on foot.

After the Ardennes offensive was over, Ninth Army attacked over the River Roer in Operation Grenade, under British 21st Army Group control. The operation was a brilliant success and, along with the British Operation Veritable, pushed the German defenders out of the Rhineland into Germany. The fighting was as intense as ever experienced in the ETO but at the end of the campaign the Germans had suffered catastrophic losses with high numbers of prisoners—as high as 52,000 men.

U.S. Ninth Army has been something of a poor relation when it comes to the analysis of the events of WWII, with far more books and column inches devoted to First and Third armies and their generals. One of the reasons for this is the character of Lt Gen William Hood Simpson, the army commander, whose diplomatic abilities—he was able to work closely with Montgomery!— were as striking as his appearance. In fact, Simpson commanded U.S. Ninth Army with great aplomb, "I have never known a commander to make better use of his staff than General Simpson," said Armistead D. Mead, his wartime G-3. Like Patton, Simpson had been in Mexico in 1916 as part of Pershing's Punitive Expedition against Pancho Villa, and had shown personal bravery in WWI in the St. Mihiel and Meuse-Argonne campaigns, earning a Silver Star and a Distinguished Service Medal. Eisenhower dubbed him a clear thinker, energetic, balanced; Monty praised his work both during the Battle of the Bulge and afterwards during the Rhineland campaign. William Vandivert/The LIFE Picture Collection/Getty Images

Opposite: *Camp Patton at Néhou on the Cotentin Peninsula remembers Third Army's sojourn here before becoming operational on August 1, 1944.*

15

Sixth SS-Panzerarmee

Dietrich's Sixth SS-Panzerarmee was the spearhead of the German assault, with the best equipment and men. Formed in fall 1944 around Paderborn, it had two SS-Panzerkorps, I (Priess) and II (Bittrich), and LXVII Infanteriekorps (Hitzfeld). With four SS-Panzer divisions (*Leibstandarte, Das Reich, Hitlerjugend,* and *Hohenstaufen*), it also had more tanks and artillery pieces than Manteuffel's Fifth Panzerarmee. The Sixth SS-Panzerarmee mustered around 270 tanks, mainly Panthers and PzKpfw IVs, but with a sizable complement of Tigers (twenty-two Tiger Is in sPzAbt 301 and twenty-two Tiger IIs of sPzAbt 506). On top of this there were just over 200 Jagdpanthers/Jagdpanzer IVs and Hetzers, over 100 StuGs, 685 guns, and nearly 350 Nebelwerfer. It would also receive later the 902nd StuG Brigade and the superheavy 380mm mortars of the 1000th (three vehicles) and 1001st (four vehicles) Sturmmörser companies. PzStuMrKp 1000 was raised in August 1944 and fought during the Warsaw Uprising PzStuMrKp 1001 (Hauptmann von Gottberg) was raised in September.

Dietrich also had Panzer Brigade 150, the special forces who were to recon the Meuse bridges, hold them until the main force arrived, and foment panic in the American lines by infiltrating English speakers in captured uniforms and vehicles (see pp. 34–35).

In spite of the hardware and the bridging units—Pioneer-Brücken Bn 655 and *Brückenkolonnen* 602, 967, 968, 403, and 406 with pontoon bridging equipment; 175, 844, 851, and 895 with girder bridges—Sixth Panzerarmee failed to get close to the Meuse, with *Hitlerjugend* finding the Elsenborn Ridge too tough a nut to crack, and then *Leibstandarte*'s Kampfgruppe Peiper held at bay by lack of fuel and "those damned engineers," who blew the bridges in front of them.

T–B: *Sixth Panzerarmee SS-Panzer division insignia:* Leibstandarte, Das Reich, Hitlerjugend, *and* Hohenstaufen.

Fifth Panzerarmee

Originally formed in Tunisia on December 2, 1942, as part of Panzerarmee Afrika, it was destroyed in the fighting in North Africa, surrendering in May 1943. On August 6, 1944, it was reconstituted from Panzergruppe West and on September 9, Manteuffel took command of the elements that escaped the Falaise Pocket and the retreat across France.

Its mission in the Ardennes was "to break through the enemy positions in the Olzheim–Gemünd sector under cover of darkness, and to thrust across the Meuse on both sides of Namur up to Brussels."

It had three corps. LXVI Infantry was to attack the Schnee Eifel before pressing on to St. Vith, and planned to cross the Meuse in the Huy–Andenne sector. LVIII Panzer (116th Pz Div) was to cross the River Our at Ouren, then advance via Houffalize to cross the Meuse in the Andenne–Namur sector. XLVII Panzer (2nd Pz Div, a weakened Panzer Lehr Div, 9th Pz Div from Christmas) was to cross the Our between Dasburg and Gemünd, bypass Clervaux, capture Bastogne, then cross the Meuse between Dinant and Givet.

The Führer Begleit Brigade (Oberst Otto-Ernst Remer) was in OKW reserve but was committed towards St. Vith when the breakthough occurred.

Opposing the Fifth Panzerarmee were U.S. 28th and 106th Infantry divisions, the former resting after heavy fighting in the Hürtgen Forest; the latter having arrived in theater in early December, replacing 2nd Inf Div in the line on December 11.

Manteuffel's army advanced deep into Allied territory, inflicting significant losses—particularly to the 28th Division's 110th Inf Regt and to the 106th's 422nd and 423rd Inf Regts which were cut off and surrendered on December 19—but was unable to break through to the Meuse and ended up in the vain attempt to take Bastogne.

T–B: *Fifth Panzerarmee Panzer division insignia: 2nd, Panzer Lehr, 9th, and 116th* (Windhund).

General Manteuffel
(1897–1978)

General der Panzertruppen Hasso von Manteuffel was a career solder whose slight build hid a charismatic and deft military brain. Scion of a Pomeranian military household, Manteuffel joined the cavalry, fighting in WWI before joining the Freikorps and then the Reichswehr. An early proponent of armored, mobile warfare, in 1939 he became a senior professor at Panzer Troop School II in Berlin-Krampnitz, before becoming commander of Schützen-Regiment 6 in 7th Panzer Division. He made his name as commander in the Grossdeutschland Division in Russia. In the Ardennes, his army made the deepest penetration, getting close to the Meuse before being halted by U.S. and British armor. Bogged down around Bastogne, after Sixth SS-Panzerarmee left the Ardennes for Hungary, Manteuffel's forces were pushed back by U.S. First and Third Armies.

Left: *Most Nebelwerfer were the towed varieties which were easily hitched to a vehicle. The Panzerwerfer 42 auf Maultier, SdKfz 4/1 seen here, was not produced in great numbers (just over 300 pairs of it and its ammunition carrier) The roof-mounted 150mm, 10-barrel rocket launcher could be traversed through 270 degrees, elevated up to 80 degrees, and was guided with a RA35 optical sight.*

Gen Brandenberger
(1892 –1955)

General der Panzertruppen Erich Brandenberger joined the Königlich Bayerische Armee in 1911, fought in World War I and afterwards joined the Freikorps. He held a variety of positions in the Reichswehr, including command of Artillery Regiment (motorized) 74, a number of staff jobs, and head of the General Staff of the Command of the Grenz-truppen Eifel in the Ardennes. In wartime, by now Generalmajor, he commanded 8th Panzer Division and then a number of Armeekorps in Russia. He took over from Eberbach after the latter was captured during the Falaise Gap battles. On August 31, 1944, he became commander of the Seventh Armee which he led until the end of the Ardennes offensive when he was dismissed. On March 26, 1945, he took over command of the Nineteenth Armee which he surrendered in Austria a few weeks later.

Above: *Gen Eric Brandenberger, commanding the Nineteenth Armee in Austria, outside his HQ at the time of his surrender at Innsbruck, Austria at 13:30 on May 15, 1945.*

Right: *Volksgrenadier armed with an StG-44.*

Seventh Armee

The southern flank of the German attack was given to the three Armeekorps of Seventh Armee—a force that sounds bigger and better than it was, lacking any significant armor and with a number of weaker, recently formed units. LXXXV Armeekorps (General der Infanterie Baptist Kniess) comprised 5th Fallschirmjäger Division, which was rebuilding after the Falaise Gap battles, and 352nd Volksgrenadier Division, which had recently been created but was almost at full strength. LXXX Armeekorps (General der Infanterie Franz Beyer) had two Volksgrenadier divisions, 212th and 276th—the latter created in September was in poor condition, whereas 212th was almost up to strength and rated as Brandenberger's best division. Finally, LIII Armeekorps (General der Kavallerie Edwin von Rothkirch) was on the southern edge of the offensive. It was tasked with crossing the Sauer and then blocking the anticipated counterattack by Third Army from the south. This was a significant role as Manteuffel's Fifth Panzerarmee hoped to have a long flank as it motored towards the Meuse. This defense was predicated in getting to its blocking positions in good time—but with insufficient bridging equipment, 212th Volksgrenadier Division, as Hugh Cole points out, took forty-eight hours to put a 16-ton bridge over the river, which in turn meant that the attack was without any heavy weapons for the first three days, so LXXX Corps didn't reach its first-day objectives until December 19. The southern shoulder quickly jammed until Christmas, when the corps was pushed back to the Sauer.

Seventh Armee's divisional insignia:
Above Left *212th VG Division;*
Above *5th FJR;*
Left *276th VG Division.*

BR XXX Corps

The British involvement in the Battle of Bulge was small but significant. The initial assault on First Army had caused if not panic then certainly significant control issues. Eisenhower—much against his better judgment—placed Field Marshal Montgomery in charge of the northern shoulder of the bulge. This certainly offended nationalistic sensibilities—and a very vocal American Press corps was bound to take it amiss—but Eisenhower knew what he was doing. Monty, for all his faults, was a professional, experienced commander of armies and reacted with calm authority. He immediately set about protecting the Meuse bridges against the threat, sealing the river line, moving XXX Corps from Holland, and building a force that comprised 6th Airborne, two infantry divisions—51st (Highland) and 53rd (Welsh)—Guards Armoured, and three armored brigades (29th, 33rd, and 34th); 43rd (Wessex) and 50th (Northumbrian) divisions were in reserve.

6th Airborne (Maj Gen Eric Bols), including 1st Canadian Para Bn, rushed to Belgium from England by boat and landed on December 22, concentrating between Dinant and Namur by December 26. It was withdrawn at the end of January. 29th Armoured Bde—23rd Hussars, 2nd Fife and Forfar Yeomanry, and 3rd Royal Tank Regiment—had been around Ypres, western Belgium training on the newly arrived Comet tanks, equipped with 17-pdrs when the attack required it to act. It immediately took back its old vehicles and headed to the front. On December 24 3RTR crossed the Meuse and supported U.S. 2nd Armd Div's attack on 2nd Panzer Division around Celles. The German tanks, short of fuel and harried by U.S. P-38 Lightnings, were halted and many were abandoned, their crews escaping on foot.

In early January the Allies counterattacked the salient, with XXX Corps involved until pulled out of the line on January 16 to prepare for the battle of the Rhineland.

Lt Gen Thomas
(1893–1972)

Lt Gen Sir Brian Gwynne Horrocks commanded XXX Corps from the end of the battle of Normandy. The corps had led the advance through Belgium, taking Brussels, before leading the ground assault during Operation Market Garden. At the end of December Monty ordered Horrocks home on sick leave. He thought he was being sacked. Monty told him: "Don't be stupid... I want you to go home and have a rest before a big battle I've got in store for you as soon as we've cleared up this mess here." His replacement was Maj Gen Gwilym Ivor Thomas, an artilleryman awarded the DSO and two MCs in WWI. He had become GOC 43rd (Wessex) Division in early 1942 and commanded it for the rest of the war. The "Yellow Devils," as the Germans called them, was one of the best Allied infantry divisions of the war. Not without his critics (the battles around Hill 112 earned him the nickname "Butcher"), Thomas proved safe pair of hands. He returned to his command when Horrocks returned at the end of January 1945.

Left: *Snow-suited men of 6th Airborne. Developed for the possible invasion of Norway, the snow suit was used extensively during the Battle of the Bulge by British and American troops.*

War Department Field Manual (FM) 100-20, Command and Employment of Air Power, 21 July 1943
(from "Air Power in the Battle of the Bulge")

"It was the successful, battle-honed model of FM Sir Bernard Law Montgomery and Air Vice Marshal Coningham that defined the principles of air support that became U.S. Army Air Corps doctrine on 21 July 1943 in FM 100-20. The missions of air power employment as spelled out in FM 100-20 were:

First priority. *To gain the necessary degree of air superiority. This will be accomplished by attacks against aircraft in the air and on the ground and against those installations that the enemy requires for the application of air power.*
Second priority. *To prevent the movement of hostile troops and supplies into the theater of operations or within the theater (air interdiction).*
Third Priority. *To participate in a combined effort of the air and ground forces, in the battle area, to gain objectives on the immediate front of the ground forces (close cooperation)."*

The Germans attacked on December 16 and not only on the ground: some 2,400 aircraft were ready to support the land forces. The problem was that the Luftwaffe in recent times had been set up to defend the Reich against Allied bombers. The liaison system between army and air force was poor and the coordination between German air defense flak units and Luftwaffe fighters was extremely poor. Operational planning, as Col William R. Carter identifies, "was as flawed as the force structure. The operational order for the attack of Heeresgruppe B toward Antwerp stated that the first priority of the Luftwaffe was 'ground support for Panzer spearheads.' Air was 'to attack the roads along the axis of advance and the preparation areas.' Only key points were to be supported due to limited air assets. Second priority was to 'attack against the airfields of the enemy tactical units close to the front.'"

The Allies, on the other hand, had been honing and developing their skills since 1943 and the battles in the North African desert. By the end of 1944 the air component of the Allies was a well-organized, skillful operation with excellent inter-Service cooperation, well-stated doctrine and operational principles. As a result, when the weather permitted, Allied fighters and fighter-bombers attacked the Germans' advancing columns and provided tactical support to the hard-pressed land forces.

The first priority—as laid out in FM 100-20—was to achieve a level of air superiority; next the air forces had to work closely with the forces on the ground to blunt the German attack; finally, the enemy's logistic apparatus had to be impaired to starve them of fuel and ammunition.

The flexibility of the leadership of the Allied air force was shown when Eisenhower adjusted his command structure, placing the northern forces under Montgomery. The commander of 2TAF, AM Coningham, put General Elwood R. "Pete" Quesada, commander of the IX TAC, in control of all the Allied air assets in the north. With Eighth Air Force attacking airfields, the light and medium bombers of the Ninth Air Force's 9th BD, XXIX TAC and the RAF's 2TAF roaming the Eifel, the battlefield itself was left to IX TAC in the north and XIX in the south.

Generalfeldmarschall Walther Model said: "Enemy number one is the hostile air force, which because of its absolute superiority tries to destroy our spearheads of attack and our artillery through fighter-bomber attacks and bomb carpets and to render movements in the rear areas impossible."

Left: *Strafing run: between December 16, 1944, and January 16, 1945, according to the Army Air Forces' official history, the Eighth and Ninth Air Forces destroyed 11,378 German transport vehicles, 1,161 tanks and other armored vehicles, 507 locomotives, 6,266 railroad cars, 472 gun positions, 974 rail cuts, 421 road cuts, and thirty-six bridges. Ground-based radar played a significant role in the battle. As Carter points out, Quesada innovated. "He used the MEW radar and the SCR-584 anti-aircraft radar in several new and unplanned ways, building an entire command and control network centered around this new technology. To assist ground-attack missions, MEW operators coordinated with SCR-584 operators to provide navigation and precise control to fighter-bombers. The wide-band MEW was used for long-range and area control, while the SCR-584, with its narrow beam, was used for close-range, precision work ... Radar operators helped fighters get under and through the weather both in the target areas and at recovery bases and validated targets by correlating ground locations with tracked fighter positions. Furthermore, IX TAC used the SCR-584 to 'blind bomb' through overcast skies such area targets as Saint Vith and to direct night aerial reconnaissance flights. As a result, the fighter-bombers controlled by the IX TAC effectively supported Allied ground forces, even in times of poor weather and confusing ground tactical situations."*

Center left: *Operation Repulse—the resupply of 101st Airborne in Bastogne—was not without danger. Heavy flak led to 19 losses—in this case, Ain't Misbehavin' crash-landed successfully near Savy.*

Below left: *Men of B Co, 506th PIR retrieve an A-4 Aerial Delivery Container full of medical supplies. Between 09:30 on December 23 and the afternoon of December 26 when the siege was broken, IX Troop Carrier Command flew 962 sorties and dropped 850 tons of supplies to the defenders.*

Operation *Bodenplatte*

Bodenplatte: the cost
(figures from Manrho & Putz)

Germany
c. 850 aircraft—mainly
Bf109G-14 or K-4s,
FW190A-8 or D-9 fighter-
bombers led out by Ju88 and
Ju188 nightfighters as
pathfinders. Some thirty-
three Gruppen deployed
from II Jagdkorps (Fighter
Corps) commanded by
Generalmajor Dietrich Peltz.
284 destroyed—sixty-seven
in air combat—with 213
pilots lost.

Allied
305 destroyed on around
twenty airfields in Belgium,
France, and Holland.
190 damaged, fifteen shot
down in air combat, and ten
damaged in air combat, with
around fourteen pilots killed.

On January 1, 1945, the Luftwaffe launched an all-out attack on the Allied air forces in the Low Countries. It had been planned to attack on same day that the ground operation was launched—December 16, 1944—but the bad weather that hid the German attacking forces also held up Operation *Bodenplatte* (Baseplate) until New Year's Day. Born of desperation, it ended an awful month for the Luftwaffe. Werner Girbig gives these figures for pilot losses over the period: December 1–16: 136 fighter pilots failed to return to base after operations; December 19–22: 83; December 23–31: 316; Operation *Bodenplatte* saw a further 255 casualties, including 170 dead and sixty-seven made PoW.

The operation certainly achieved some surprise, but was ultimately a failure. Around 500 Allied aircraft were damaged or destroyed—mostly on the ground—but replaced within a week. Allied aircrew casualties were also small in number, because the majority were empty aircraft sitting on the ground. The Germans, however, lost many pilots they could not readily replace. To add insult to injury, a number of the Luftwaffe losses (probably around thirty) were to their own Flak defenses who were unaware of the operation.

Bodenplatte was the last large-scale strategic offensive operation mounted by the Luftwaffe during the war and is commonly regarded as its death ride. Shortly after, on January 22 at the Luftwaffe Club in Berlin the so-called "Mutiny of the Aces" took place in which Peltz in particular, and to a lesser extent Göring were excoriated by their top pilots. As one can imagine, it did not go down well.

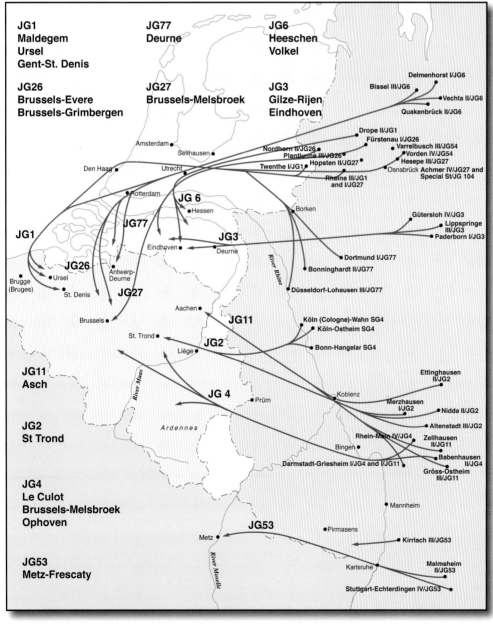

Opposite, Above: *This Fw 190A-8/R2 (Wk-Nr. 681497) was flown by 5./JG 4's Gefreiter Walter Wagner during Operation* Bodenplatte *on January 1, 1945. Attacking the Allied airfield at St. Trond, in Belgium, on what was only his third ever combat mission, Wagner was forced to land near his target when the engine of his fighter cut out after being hit by ground fire. (via Eddie Nielinger)*

Opposite, Below: *P-47 Thunderbolts supplied effective air cover and close support over the battlefield.* Bodenplatte *saw at least forty-five destroyed and around twenty damaged.*

Above: *The aftermath of Operation* Bodenplatte *at Eindhoven—No 137 Sqn Typhoon JR260/SF-Z, in which Flt Sgt Lance Burrows was fatally wounded, shares the apron with the remains of an Anson. The latter was possibly Wg Cdr Erik Haabjorn's aircraft that he had flown in from the Central Fighter Establishment at Tangmere. (E. Haabjorn)*

Artillery

There's no doubt that American artillery played a massive role in the defeat of the Ardennes offensive. In each of three basic requirements of field artillery—gunnery, movement, and communication—it outperformed its rival, the latter being easier for the Americans who could use fixed lines.

In gunnery, U.S. massed fire benefited from fire direction centers (FDC) at battalion level and the accuracy of its time-on-target (TOT) fire missions in which the guns of all batteries are concentrated on one target, with the projectiles programmed to arrive on target at the same moment. This was particularly effective on the Elsenborn Ridge, where four divisions defended the northern shoulder and V Corps Artillery Commander, Brig. Gen. Helmick, ordered 2nd Division Artillery to coordinate the fires of all four divisions. On the 22nd, the 2nd Division fired sixty-three TOTs—mostly with forty-four guns per mission—and the enemy was kept at bay. Air observation also helped targeting. The Germans could only dream of such consistency, and in the face of Allied air superiority, air observation was almost completely out of the question.

In terms of mobility, American artillery was streets ahead of its adversary. Apart from the Germans' acute shortage of gasoline, their field artillery was not able to keep up with the advancing Panzers because most of it was horse-drawn.

American and German divisional artillery was very similar, having followed the same developmental pattern during the 1930s, but fighting on the Eastern Front had seen the Germans buy into rocket artillery, the *Werfer*, a multiple-tube rocket launcher. As well as being easy to produce, it was also easy to transport. These weapons lacked the accuracy and fire control features, but they were more mobile than many other German artillery pieces. As Hugh Cole says, "There is no doubt that the German artillery helped the assault waves forward during the rupture of the American forward defensive positions. It is equally clear that the German artillery failed to keep pace with the subsequent advance, nor did it come forward rapidly enough to assist substantially in the reduction of those American points of resistance which had been left in the rear of attacking echelons."

This Page: *30th Inf Div's 113th Field Artillery Bn was one of four divisional artillery battalions and consisted of twelve x 155mm howitzers. The late Dr. Van Heely was Battalion Assistant S3 in the 113th. Resting after the River Roer battles when the offensive began, the unit was ordered south toward Eupen to prepare for a counterattack to the southeast. However, the advance of Kampfgruppe Peiper changed everything. At 16:30 on December 17 the division moved off by combat teams; en route, the leading combat team—the 117th Infantry—was ordered to Malmédy. The next morning, further orders: one battalion was to go to Stavelot to stop the Germans from advancing north of the Amblève River. CO of the 117th was Walter K. Johnson, who had been promoted colonel in October. He hurried his 1st Bn toward Stavelot, deploying his 2nd Bn on the ridge between Stavelot and Malmédy, and put the 3rd Battalion into Malmédy. It was too late. On the morning of December 18 the Germans attacked and took Stavelot ... and reports came in of German armor moving north from Trois-Ponts in the direction of La Gleize and Stoumont. At this critical juncture, the 30th Division did what it had done at Mortain: it took the fight to the enemy, retaking Stavelot (thanks to the timely arrival of air support) and destroying the bridge and thereby cutting Peiper's lines of communications and logistics. His force would come up against the rest of 30th Division at Stoumont and be held up long enough for 82nd Airborne to join the battle. Heavy fighting saw the Kampfgruppe knocked back and, out of fuel, Peiper and his men abandoned their vehicles and melted away heading back to their lines.*

Opposite, Top: *Heely's photo of the Baugnez crossroads where the Malmédy massacre took place.*

Opposite, Center: *A howitzer of B Battery, 113th FA Bn, in a camouflaged position at Ster, just north of Stavelot.*

Opposite, Below: *No 2 gun of A Battery in full recoil—another view from Ster.*

Above: *Each U.S. armored division had three battalions of M7 105mm HMCs, giving them a great deal of mobile artillery support.*

Center Right: *Members of the 489th Field Artillery 7th Armd Div, load a pile of shells on a truck after supporting the infantry in their attack on the high ground near St. Vith on January 25.*

Below Right: *M114 155mm howitzer of A Battery, 113th FA Bn having moved to Recht, northeast of St. Vith, January 1945. The M114 used two-part ammunition (a projectile and a separate bagged propellant charge). While it mostly fired HE, it could also fire illumination, smoke or white phosphorus shells. Over 4,000 of the M1 and M1A1 were produced. The howitzer had a range of 16,000 yards firing HE; the smoke would go out to 9,700 yards, and the illumination to 7,000. A good crew (usually eleven men) could fire forty rounds a minute—with great accuracy. It served with the U.S. Army into the Vietnam War.*

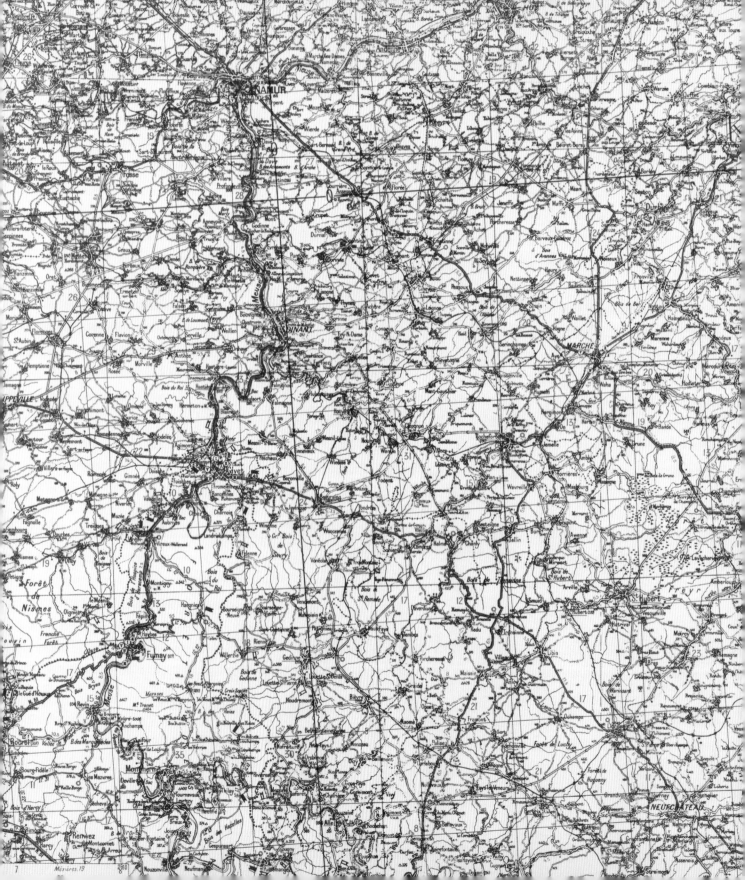

1 THE GERMAN PLAN

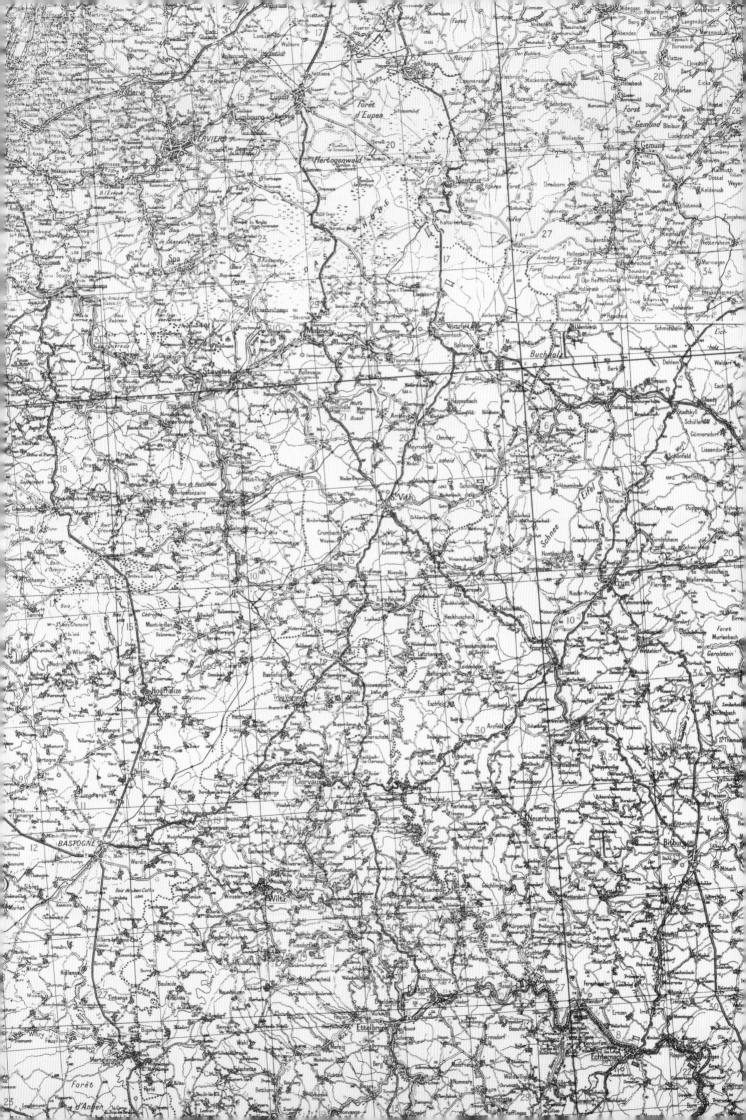

Hitler's Masterstroke?

"When the disproportion of Power is so great that no limitation of our own object can ensure us safety from catastrophe ... forces will, or should, be concentrated in one desperate blow." Hitler always prided himself on his military reading and histories of Frederick II and the writings of Carl von Clausewitz were key to his military strategy. This quote from *On War* sums up well Hitler's rationale for an offensive that was very much his own idea.

The Ardennes had proved to be the scene of one of Hitler's greatest strategic successes in 1940. Is it so surprising that he tried again? The enemy front in the Ardennes was very thinly manned with units that were either green or recovering from hard fighting. Hitler's main hope for the attack was that it would strike the seam between the British and American armies and lead to political as well as military disharmony between the Allies. There's no doubt that ill-feeling did exist between the two allies but it was always well handled by the top people: it's no surprise that Eisenhower went on to become president. He showed immense skill in keeping the egos of his generals and—more importantly the nationalistic Press corps—in check. Hitler hoped that he could split the Allies, isolate British 21st Army Group, and defeat it before moving over to attack the Americans.

Hugh Cole cites four other reasons for the choice of the Ardennes:

- The proximity of the jump-off line to a solid strategic objective (Antwerp) which should have allowed the distance to be covered quickly, even in bad weather.
- The configuration of the area was such that the ground for maneuver was limited and so would require the use of relatively few divisions.
- The terrain to the east of the breakthrough sector selected was very heavily wooded and offered cover against Allied air observation and attack during the build-up for the assault.
- An attack to regain the initiative in this particular area would erase the enemy ground threat to the Ruhr.

Hitler's generals suggested a simpler plan whose objective would be an encirclement of the U.S. forces east of the Meuse and their defeat, thus providing a breathing space to construct a defense of the Reich. But Hitler was adamant and the attack date was set.

Above: *Adolf Hitler was fifty-six and a half years old when the Ardennes campaign started. In spite of his increasingly poor health—advanced syphilis and Parkinson's disease have both been offered as reasons—he was still as autocratic as ever, and few of his generals or associates would argue with him. The successes of the early war were far away, and at the turn of the new year, with the Allies advancing on every front, his decision-making grew increasingly irrational. Far from a masterstroke, Hitler's grandiose plan to split the Allies, thus causing them to sue for peace so that he could concentrate on the Eastern Front, was a pipe-dream. However, in one area his plan was successful: amassing the troops for the attack saw the Germans achieve complete surprise. Initially, that surprise and the weather led to territorial gains and some disquiet to Eisenhower and his headquarters.*

Right: *In the end, Hitler underrated the staying power of the Allied soldiers, the strength of the alliance, and the abilities of their generals.*

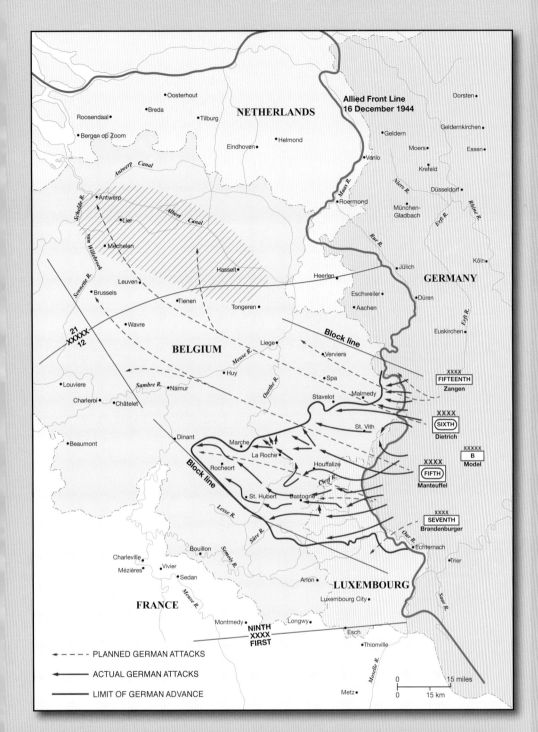

Allied Front Line
16 December 1944

NETHERLANDS

GERMANY

BELGIUM

Block line

Block line

FRANCE

LUXEMBOURG

XXXX
FIFTEENTH
Zangen

XXXX
SIXTH
Dietrich

XXXXX
B
Model

XXXX
FIFTH
Manteuffel

XXXX
SEVENTH
Brandenburger

- - - PLANNED GERMAN ATTACKS

ACTUAL GERMAN ATTACKS

LIMIT OF GERMAN ADVANCE

0   15 miles
0   15 km

von Rundstedt
(1875 –1953)

Generalfeldmarschall Karl Rudolf Gerd von Rundstedt was born into a Prussian aristocratic family in Aschersleben, Germany. He entered the Prussian Army in 1892 and in World War I served mainly as a staff officer. In the interwar years, he continued his military career, reaching the rank of Generaloberst) before retiring in 1938. Rundstedt remained in the army after the war and was active in Germany's secret rearmament both before and after Hitler came to power. He was recalled at the beginning of World War II and commanded Army Group South in the invasion of Poland and Army Group A in France. During the invasion of the Soviet Union, he commanded Army Group South. Relieved of command in December 1941, he was made Oberbefehlshaber West (OBW—Commander-in-Chief in the West) in 1942 and was subsequently dismissed after the battle of Normandy ended in July 1944. He returned to the OBW role in September and directed the Ardennes offensive—it is called the von Rundstedt Offensive in some books. He continued as OBW until his final dismissal by Hitler in March 1945. Rundstedt was aware of the various plots to depose Hitler, but refused to support them. After the war, he was charged with war crimes, but did not face trial.

29

German Resources

Above: *The Third Reich had a love affair with heavy tanks—as exemplified here by the PzKpfw Tiger Ausf. B, often referred to as the King Tiger. The trouble, however, was that heavy tanks were not the best AFVs to fight in the Ardennes. With few metaled roads, numerous small rivers and streams to cross, and weak bridges, the lumbering 77-ton monsters struggled to keep up with Peiper's Kampfgruppe—so much so that most were abandoned. It was the Panther and PzKpfw IV that proved to be the workhorses of the panzer divisions in the Ardennes.*

Note: *The "Fkl" is short for Funklenk—radio-controlled—because the unit was originally equipped with Goliath demolition vehicles.*

By December 15, the Germans had secretly assembled a large force that was poised to attack American units who were if not totally unprepared, then certainly not expecting action. There had been no Ultra intelligence forewarning the Allies: the Germans had been careful to maintain security and use couriers rather than radio or field telephones. There had been reports of a build-up of forces, but no one on the Allied side expected an attack by thirteen infantry, two airborne units, and nine Panzer divisions, with another three infantry divisions and a Panzer division added after the offensive began.

However, as Maj James L. Kennedy outlines, while this formation gave the Germans good-looking force ratios of 2:1 in manpower and 3:1 in tanks and assault guns, the German armies had significant shortcomings. They were desperately short of fuel, and while the SS units were reasonably well provided with vehicles, some units had less than half their allocation. Cole identifies one unit with as many as sixty different types of transportation vehicles, which meant that spare parts would always be a problem. On top of this, artillery prime movers and recovery vehicles were in limited supply as were engineer equipment and vehicles.

The Ardennes in winter was a difficult place for fuel conservation: snow and steep valleys increased fuel consumption and meant that resupply was crucial. KG Peiper is a good example—particularly as hold-ups at Losheimergraben saw the Kampfgruppe consume fuel faster than expected and, consequently, request fuel earlier than planned. Peiper captured some 50,000 gallons of American fuel at Büllingen but missed the huge dump on the Francorchamps road out of Stavelot. The bridge there became crucial to the Kampfgruppe's survival as it was through here that all Peiper's resupply was channeled. The loss of Stavelot, in spite of continued attempts to retake the town, meant that Peiper's position in La Gleize could not be resupplied and he eventually had to abandon his vehicles and escape on foot. The same thing happened to the advanced armor of Fifth Panzerarmee as it neared the Meuse. When U.S. 2nd Armd Div attacked, their opponents were running on fumes.

The short supply did not end with fuel. Ammunition was also wanting, as was bridging material. Once the American combat engineers—in particular the 291st at Trois-Ponts and Lienne Creek at Habiémont—had destroyed the bridges in front of him, Peiper, without a bridging train, was unable to proceed.

The figures for German tank and artillery strengths are difficult to cover precisely. Take the *bête noire* of every GI, the "ubiquitous" Tiger—ubiquitous because just as every artillery piece was an 88mm, so every German tank was a Tiger. In fact, as *Sledgehammers* identifies, there were no more than eighty-six Tiger IIs at the start of the Ardennes Offensive, KG Peiper having forty-five in SS-sPzAbt 501, and Fifth Panzerarmee's sPzAbt 506 having forty-one. During the battle, between December 17, 1944, and January 13, 1945, sPzAbt 506 lost six in combat and another to air attack. SS-sPzAbt 501 also lost six in combat and abandoned another nine.

There were a few Tiger Is, too. *Schwere Panzerkompanie Hummel* became sPzAbt 506's 4th Kompanie with eight Tiger Is. When the company left sPzAbt 506's strength, they had only five. Also, sPzAbt (Tiger/Fkl— *see note opposite*) 301 with twenty-nine Tigers was attached to the 9th Pz Div. Allied air interdiction of rail lines made this link-up impossible.

On the other side, the Allies also had their problems because their supply lines were at full stretch. However, they benefited from the manufacturing power of Britain and its empire, and—more significantly— the United States. Tanks and equipment were replaced quickly. On the personnel replacement front, however, the huge supply of soldiers from the United States ensured that U.S. servicemen outnumbered those of the other Allies. The table above, using figures from Trevor Dupuy, shows well just how quickly the Allies dominated the numbers game, rapidly rushing reinforcements and replacements to the front.

	Allied		Axis	
	16 Dec	16 Jan	16 Dec	16 Jan
Men	228,741	700,520	406,342	383,016
Tanks	483	2,428	557	216
TDs/asslt guns	499	1,912	667	414
Other AFVs	1,921	7,079	1,261	907
ATk/artillery	971	3,181	4,224	3,256
Armd divs	2	8	7	8
Armd bdes			2	1
Inf divs	6	22	13	16
Inf bdes			2	

Top: *The Allied strategic bombing campaign, and the loss of territories in the last six months of 1944, severely affected motor gasoline production—from a high of 200,000 tons in spring 1944 to 50,000 tons in December. This shortage of fuel caused severe problems during the offensive and meant that many division commanders issued orders to capture Allied fuel dumps where possible. Peiper captured a dump at Büllingen, but as he neared the fuel dump on the Stavelot–Francorchamps road, it was destroyed rather than let it fall into his hands (although, in fact, he was not aware of its existence).*

The Weather

The German offensive took place during the worst winter in Europe for fifty years. "Weather is a weapon the German army used with success, especially in the Ardennes offensive," said von Rundstedt, the German commander-in-chief in the west, following his capture five months later. On December 16, as the weather map (above left) shows, the fronts and pressure centers at the start of the battle led to a southerly flow over the Ardennes and the airmass was modified cold polar maritime. With the prolonged airflow from the Atlantic, plenty of moisture was available to support the fog and stratus that continued for several days (below left). As the front that was over England on the 16th approached Belgium, rain began. Heavy mists hung over the forest.

Around December 18, a thaw set in, slowing the movement of the German Panzers, and the fog began to develop openings, allowing the Allied fighter-bombers to become active—something that had an immediate effect, for example at Cheneux where strafing knocked out a Panther and impeded KG Peiper sufficiently for the 291st Engineers to blow the bridge over the Lienne at Habiémont. And on the 19th, the fog lifted at Noville in time for Team Desobry's tanks and TDs to see and stop 2nd Panzer Division's attack.

On the 20th and 21st, the ground at higher elevations began to freeze in patches, leaving stretches of the Ardennes roads slippery and muddy, so that Sixth Panzerarmee bogged down in the muddy narrow roads—particularly the heavyweight Tiger IIs. In the south, Fifth Panzerarmee was held up around Bastogne by fog and snow. Along the German supply roads beyond the Eifel, the snow fell continuously and the lack of motorized snowplows or means of gritting the roads meant resupply operations were well-nigh impossible.

The weather broke for five days from December 23 (above right) as a high pressure area extended east–west across Northern Europe from England to Russia. Cold polar continental air flowed into the Ardennes and completely modified the air over the combat zone (below right). Decreasing cloudiness allowed Allied air power to break the back of the German offensive. Bombers and fighter-bombers headed towards the front.

The Bastogne air drop began with the first of the carriers dropping its six para-packs at 11:50. On December 24, 160 planes dropped supplies; on the 25th the weather was worse, but eleven gliders brought in a medical team and fuel; and on the 26th, 289 planes flew the Bastogne run. There's no doubt that the break in the weather materially assisted the defense of this important transport hub—although it must not be forgotten that it also allowed the Luftwaffe to operate, and their bombers caused severe damage in night attacks on the beleaguered town.

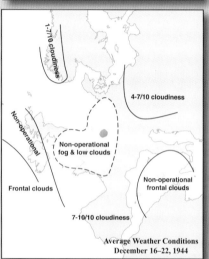

December 16, 1944
1200Z

Average Weather Conditions
December 16–22, 1944

1 The photos on this spread show the Arctic conditions under which much of the fighting took place. Trench foot was a perennial hazard for men living in foxholes in these conditions —the arrival of shoe pacs (felt insoles and Arctic or ski wool socks) helped, as did the purchase of British waterpoof ponchos and snow suits.

Weather during the Battle of the Bulge *(Marvin D. Kays)*

December 1944

16 Very low cloud and fog patches. Visibilities poor. Light rain.

17 Overcast clouds, bases 1,000–2,000ft, with intermittent rain. Visibility 3–5 miles.

18 Overcast clouds, bases 300–600ft, with light intermittent rain, becoming 500–1,000ft broken during late afternoon. Visibility 2–6 miles. Also, fog patches in the southern sector.

19 Foggy conditions all day. Visibility less than 100yd.

20 Foggy all day. Visibility less than 100yd.

21 Foggy all day. Visibility less than 100yd.

22 Overcast from 300–500ft, with light intermittent rain and snow. Visibility 500–1,000yd, reduced to less than 100yd in precipitation.

23 Fog and stratus in morning, with visibility 500–1,500yd, improving in afternoon to scattered clouds with visibility 2–4 miles.

24 Clear. Visibility 3–5 miles.

25 Clear, except for fog patches in the morning. Visibility 1,000–2,000yd, becoming 2–4 miles in the afternoon.

26 Clear, visibility 1–3 miles, except 1,000yd in fog patches.

27 Clear, except for ground fog. Visibility 500–2,000yd in fog, increasing to 2 miles in afternoon.

28 Fog and stratus, bases of stratus 100–400ft. Visibility 100–1,000yd.

29 Fog and stratus, bases of stratus 300–700ft. Visibility 200–500yd.

30 Broken to overcast clouds at 2,000–5,000ft, lowering to 500–1,000ft in precipitation during afternoon. Visibility 1,000–3,000yd, reduced to 500–1,000yd in patchy fog.

31 Broken clouds with snow showers. Visibility 3–5 miles, restricted to 1,000–2,000yd in snow showers.

January 1945

1 Clear to scattered clouds with visibility 3–5 miles, except 1–2 miles in patchy fog/haze.

2 Scattered to broken clouds becoming 500–1,000ft broken to overcast with light rain in the afternoon. Visibility 1–2 miles, except less than 1 mile in fog and rain

3 Foggy conditions in morning, 200–300ft overcast during afternoon. Visibility less than 50yd in morning, becoming 1,000–1,500yd in afternoon.

4 Overcast with bases 100–500ft with snow. Visibility 1 mile, except 100yd in snow.

5 1,000–2,000ft broken clouds with snow showers. Visibility 3–5 miles, except less than 500yd in patchy fog.

6 Fog with visibility 50–200yd, improving to 500–1,000yd during afternoon.

7 Fog in morning becoming 300–900ft broken to overcast during the afternoon. Visibility 500–1,000yd in fog, improving to 2–4 miles during afternoon, except 1 mile at 500–1000ft, snow showers.

8 Broken to overcast at 500–1,000ft, with heavy snow showers. Visibility 2–4 miles, except 1 mile in snow showers.

9 Overcast at 500–1,000ft, with visibility 1–2 miles in snow showers.

10 Small amounts of clouds and fog. Visibility 100–200yd, locally less than 50yd.

11 Fog with visibility 100–500yd, improving to 500–1,500yd in the afternoon.

12 Overcast at 300–600ft, with light snow. Clouds becoming scattered in afternoon. Visibility 500–1,000yd, except less than 500yd in local areas.

13 Foggy conditions with scattered clouds. Visibility 500–1,000yd, except less locally.

14 Clear to scattered clouds. Visibility 2–4 miles, restricted in local areas to 1–2 miles in fog and haze.

15 Foggy with visibility less than 500yd, becoming 800–1,500yd in afternoon.

16 Foggy in morning, becoming clear in afternoon. Visibility 500–1,500yd, becoming 3–5 miles during afternoon.

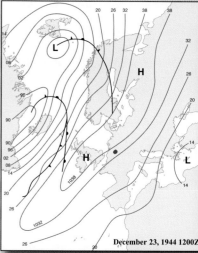

December 23, 1944 1200Z

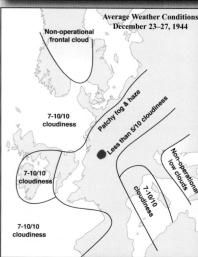

Average Weather Conditions December 23–27, 1944

Non-operational frontal cloud

Patchy fog & haze

Less than 5/10 cloudiness

7-10/10 cloudiness

Non-operational low clouds

7-10/10 cloudiness

7-10/10 cloudiness

7-10/10 cloudiness

2 Snow impeded traffic on the Germans' main supply roads and their horse-drawn snowplows were insufficient for the demand. And when the snow thawed, the mud became a consistent hazard.

3 Cold weather clothing was thin on the ground, and heavy overcoats were often discarded in battle.

4 Snow grounds an artillery liaison aircraft of the 422nd FA Bn, 3rd Armd Div.

Special Operations

Operation *Greif* (Griffin) under SS-Obersturmbannführer Otto Skorzeny consisted of two distinct missions. First, the Stielau Commandos, masquerading as American soldiers, were to infiltrate into the rear areas, conduct reconnaissance of the routes, place the bridge targets under surveillance, and spread confusion through acts of sabotage. Second, Panzer Brigade 150 would follow immediately behind the lead spearheads of I SS-Panzerkorps—1st SS-Panzer, 12th SS-Panzer, and 12th Volksgrenadier divisions—to infiltrate ahead at a suitable moment to hold the Meuse bridges open.

By wearing American uniforms they would give up their protected status as prisoners of war and, if captured, would face execution as spies. During the planning stages of the operation, it was expected that *Greif* units would be fully English-speaking and equipped with U.S. equipment. However, both a suitable number of English speakers and sufficient U.S. vehicles were hard to come by, and in the event, Panzer Brigade 150 in fact consisted of five German Panthers visually modified to resemble American M10 tank destroyers, five StuG assault guns, six armored scout cars, and six APCs. Added to this were four American scout cars and five armored half-tracks, all painted olive drab and adorned with white stars.

The Stielau Commando units fared better, and had almost two dozen jeeps but fewer than 150 competent English speakers. Raised under complete secrecy, the cat was let out of the bag as early as December 16 when a note distributed within the 62nd Volksgrenadier Division was captured near Heckhuscheid outlining the recognition signals, the use of American vehicles, equipment, and uniforms, and even the three routes the *Greif* forces would use. Nevertheless, the Stielau Commandos were to prove the most successful of the special operations. A total of nine teams went out: four reconnaissance, two demolition, and three lead teams, totaling forty-four men. One of these teams directly assisted the advance of Kampfgruppe Peiper by neutralizing the prepared demolitions on Stavelot bridge and so allowing it to be captured intact.

Below: *Both sides made use of captured equipment. It could be risky when coming into contact with troops from one's own side, but there are stories about the use of "Judas goats" or wolves in lamb's clothing—at least twice around Manhay German columns were led by captured M4s and were able to advance close to U.S. positions. Here, near Faymonville, a soldier examines an M8 Beutepanzer (lit: trophy tank) that had been captured and used by the Germans.*

Below Right: *The infiltration of Allied lines by special forces wearing American military uniforms was not as widespread as the fear and rumor that abounded. Cole mentions a jeep of such saboteurs captured by a British post at Dinant, and we know that a number of Operation Greif men were captured and executed. The idea spread among Allied troops, however, and there were many instances of returning patrols having problems with nervous sentries. The problem led to traffic controls and some disruption— as here, where military police attached to the 84th Inf Div halt and interrogate traffic at a vital crossroads directly north of Marche at Baillonville.*

The commandos remained at the front until the unit was eventually withdrawn and disbanded at the end of January 1945. Of the forty-four commandos sent through the American lines, according to Skorzeny eight failed to return: one was a firefight casualty, the other seven were executed by the Americans as spies. Although eighteen German soldiers were tried and executed as spies, Skorzeny claimed after the war that the majority of them were not part of Operation *Greif*, but just unlucky.

Panzer Brigade 150 failed to accomplish its primary mission—the seizure intact of a bridge over the Meuse River—because it never got near. Instead, it was used conventionally in an abortive attack on Malmédy.

The other special operation was Operation *Stösser* (it means auk in English), an airdrop under the command of a veteran of the battle of Crete, Oberst von der Heydte. Ill-conceived from the outset, with little planning time, virtually no time for training, inexperienced aircrew and paratroopers many of whom had never even practice-dropped (save for a hard core of 150 men from FJR6), *Stösser* was a disaster. Some 112 transports dropped around 1,300 paras in a snowstorm. Von der Heydte eventually collected around 300 men together and awaited the arrival of 12th SS-Panzer Division around the Belle-Croix crossroads. When they didn't turn up, the unit withdrew towards enemy lines: only about a third got back.

Above Left: *Howard Brodie's graphic drawing of a "Greif" commando's execution. He worked for* Yank *magazine during the war.*

Above: *Not all Germans in U.S. uniforms were spies. Some were just cold. Justice was often rough, however, and raised the rumor among Germans that the Americans were practicing a no-prisoners regime.*

Below Left: *A number of Operation Greif commandos were captured and executed as spies for being dressed in U.S. uniforms. This one is Unteroffizier Manfred Pernass.*

Below: *Panzer Brigade 150 Panther disguised as an M10.*

2 SIXTH SS-PANZERARMEE

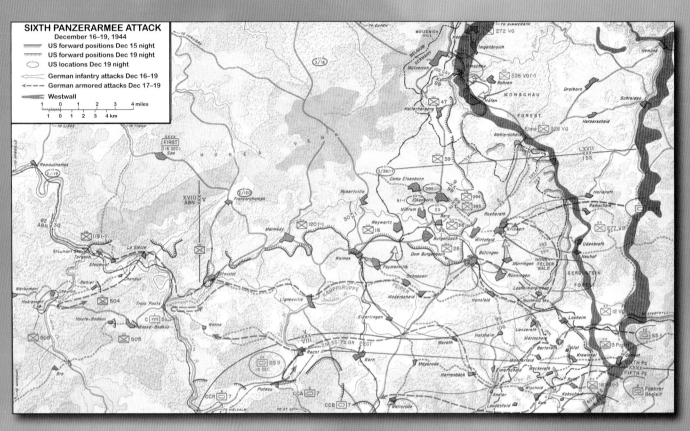

SIXTH PANZERARMEE ATTACK
December 16–19, 1944

- US forward positions Dec 15 night
- US forward positions Dec 19 night
- US locations Dec 19 night
- German infantry attacks Dec 16–19
- German armored attacks Dec 17–19
- Westwall

Above: *The northern arm of the offensive struck the Elsenborn Ridge, where three U.S. infantry divisions—the 1st, 2nd, and 99th—bore the brunt of the fighting. The crucial northern shoulder saw* Hitlerjugend *held on Elsenborn Ridge by the U.S. 1st Inf Div and* Leibstandarte *in the valleys to the west by 30th Inf and 82nd Airborne.*

This photo: *1st Division memorial on the roundabout on the road from Büllingen to Bütgenbach.*

Above and Below: *Scheid railway bridge over the Malmédy–Stadtkyll railroad line had been blown during the German retreat. Today, the line is a cycle path (below). Peiper's armored column crossed the tracks here at around 14:00 on the 16th; bridge-building delayed the Kampfgruppe. The replacement bridge was in place only around 16:00 allowing trucks and other vehicles to make their way across the border. Note the Flak 38 20mm gun providing AA defense (below right).*

The northern arm of the German offensive was entrusted to Sixth SS-Panzerarmee's I SS-Panzerkorps, spearheaded by 12th SS-Panzer Division *Hitlerjugend* and 1st SS-Panzer Division *Leibstandarte*. They attacked towards the Meuse, around seventy miles away, along *Rollbahnen*—routes along the best possible roads from which slower units, horse-drawn equipment, and soldiers on foot were banned. The most northerly, *Hitlerjugend*'s main thrust was aimed for the river crossing at Aigremont through Büllingen, Malmédy, and Spa. Their right (northern flank) was supposed to be protected by LXVII Armeekorps under Generalleutnant Otto Hitzfeld. His 272nd and 326th Volksgrenadier Divisions made few inroads around Monshau. On their left, the two VG divisions, 276th and 12th, were supposed to clear the way for *Hitlerjugend* but also ran into trouble and couldn't clear a path through the twin villages of Krinkelt and Rocherath. *Hitlerjugend* itself also had difficulties, coming up against the U.S. 99th Inf Div—a new unit untested in combat—along the Elsenborn Ridge. The 99th's 394th Regiment put up a stern fight for the Losheimergraben crossroads and delayed the advance by a day. South of *Hitlerjugend*, KG Peiper of *Leibstandarte* had got off to a slow start, thanks to bridging problems, but once it got going advanced steadily through Losheim, took Büllingen and moved towards Wirtzfeld.

Above: *German Westwall dragon teeth antitank defenses built in 1939—the border runs through the Leibstandarte attack area.*

Right: *Memorial at Losheimergraben to the action of 1/394th Inf Regt of U.S. 99th Div here on December 16.*

Below: *The Rollbahns gave* Hitlerjugend *the three northerly and* Leibstandarte *the two southerly tracks: Rollbahn D shared by KG Peiper, first, and KG Sandig. KG Hansen was first on Rollbahn E, followed by KG Knittel. Peiper said postwar: "I decided that my column would be about 25km long, and the vehicles would proceed at medium speed. It was impossible for the vehicles in the rear to overtake those in the front because of the bad roads ... all combat elements had to be in the front of the column ... "*

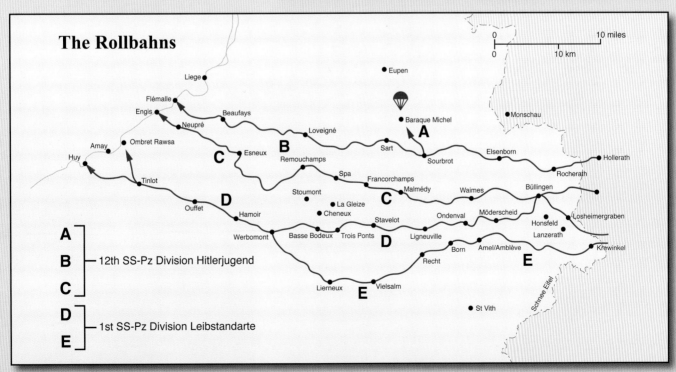

The Rollbahns

A ⎫
B ⎬ 12th SS-Pz Division Hitlerjugend
C ⎭

D ⎫
  ⎬ 1st SS-Pz Division Leibstandarte
E ⎭

1. I&R Platoon dug-in positions 18 infantrymen and 4 artillerymen
2. Separate bunker with 3 I&R men
3. Route of FJR9 of 3rd FJR Division
4. House from which a little girl ran out to warn Paratroop officer
5. Direction of repeated attacks
6. Route and direction of final attack at dusk
7. Cafe Palm
8. Schur House
9. Christen House. C Bty/372st FA Bn obs post
10. School. A Co/820th TD Bn CP
11. 2nd Pl and Recon Pl/A Co/820th TD Bn sleeping quarters
12. Scholzen House. I&R/394th OP
13. Cafe Scholzen
14. Schugens House
15. Towards Losheim
16. Road used by KG Peiper
17. Road to Losheimergraben. Blown bridge over deep RR cutting
18. Three men cut off; later captured at RR cutting.

From the Hatlem Collection files of the U.S. Army Military HistoryInstitute. Coding and key by R.H. Byers.

Above: *The I&R (Intelligence & Reconnaissance) Platoon of 394th Regiment, 99th Inf Div, consisted of two nine-man squads and a seven-man HQ section. On December 10, the platoon was ordered to a position near Lanzerath, a village of twenty-three houses and a church. They improved the foxholes left by the previous unit, digging them deeper and covering them with pine logs. They were attacked by 3rd Fallschirmjäger Division, destroyed in the Falaise pocket but brought up to strength with replacements from the 22nd, 51st, and 53rd Luftwaffe Field Regiments. The assault started on December 16 with an artillery barrage lasting from 05:30 to 07:00, which knocked out telephone lines. The platoon commander, 1Lt Lyle Bouck, was told to 'Hold at all costs!' From an OP in a house on the eastern side of the village Bouck watched 500 Germans heading toward them. As the enemy force moved through the town and in front of their positions, a girl came out of a house and pointed in their general direction. The Americans thought she had given their position away and fired on the Germans, although—as discovered more than fifty years later—that was not the case. Two platoons of 2. Kompanie I/FJR9, 3rd FJR Division, attacked, were repulsed, and continued to mount attacks until dusk when Fusilier Regiment 27 of 12th Volksgrenadier Division outflanked the American unit and forced them to surrender. The Germans reported sixteen killed, sixty-three wounded, and thirteen missing in action.*

Above: *Shellcases from the 105mm guns of the 38th FA Bn, assigned to 2nd Inf Div, litter the snowy landscape. The battalion fired more than 5,000 rounds on December 18 during the defense of Krinkelt and Rocherath.*

Left: *One of the defenders of Elsenborn Ridge.*

Opposite, Below: *Memorial to the battle by 99th Inf Div's I&R Platoon at Lanzerath who held up the German advance for a day, much to the irritation of Peiper, who turned away from Elsenborn and headed toward Stavelot instead.*

The German attack planned to bypass the Elsenborn Ridge to the south, but the ridge had to be neutralized—and to do that the so-called twin villages of Rocherath and Krinkelt had to be taken. 277th VG Division was given the task but its first attack failed. On December 18 they tried again, reinforced by the 25th PzGr Regt, an assault gun, and a tank battalion. Aided by 741st Tank Battalion, 2nd Inf Div held off the Germans until the villages were evacuated on the 19th. Five Medals of Honor were awarded for the battle, including that of Pfc William A. Soderman of Coy K, 9th Infantry, 2nd Inf Div who, armed with a bazooka, defended a key road junction near Rocherath, Belgium, on December 17, knocking out at least three PzKpfw V Panthers.

Above Right and Right: Two knocked-out Panthers of I.SS-Panzer Regiment 12 in Krinkelt. On December 18 elements of 99th Inf Div, reinforced by 2nd Inf, attacked in fog. The Panthers were easy meat for the bazooka teams.

Below, Left and Right: Memorials to two of the three main units involved in the defense: the "Battle Babes" of 99th Inf Div (**left**) and the 2nd Inf Div (**right**). Both are opposite the church in Krinkelt which is today completely changed from its wartime appearance (**Opposite, Below Left and Right**).

Above: *C Coy, 16th Inf Regt, 1st Inf Div. The Big Red One had been sent to a rest camp on December 12, but was ordered to Camp Elsenborn when the German offensive began. The 16th took up positions near Robertville and Weywertz. From there the regiment spent nearly a month engaged in firefights with 12th SS-Panzer and 3rd FJR Divisions before moving onto the offensive.*

Left: *A Panther of 12th Pz Regt burns outside Krinkelt on December 18.*

1 *Troops of the 26th Infantry Regiment, 1st Inf Div, reposition an antitank gun near Bütgenbach. The Big Red One reached Camp Elsenborn on the morning of December 17, just as KG Peiper reached Büllingen.*

2 and 3 *A truck of 372nd FA Bn, 99th Inf Div, leaves Wirtzfeld on December 17, with an M10 covering the retreat.*

4, 5, and 6 *The attacks on Elsenborn Ridge were defended stoutly, assisted by brilliant artillery work. In the end, unable to advance, 12th SS-Panzer Division headed south for redeployment under Fifth Panzerarmee.*

7 *Sturmpanzer-Abteilung 217— consisting of around eight Sturmpanzer 43 Brummbär assault guns—supported Hitlerjugend and 12th VGD in their attack, reaching Dom Bütgenbach on December 21. The photo, taken from a cine film, is said to show the Abteilung OC, Oberlt Josef Gauglitz. Note his Hensoldt Wetzlar 10x50 binoculars. Ullstein Bild via Getty Images*

8 *Map from the 1st Division memorial—a slightly different perspective to the maps at 4, 5, 6, it shows the location of the memorial.*

9 and 10 *1/26th Infantry head under a destroyed viaduct en route for Bütgenbach. On the outskirts of the village, it carried a rail line from Weywertz to Losheimergraben.*

On December 16 the front erupted as an artillery bombardment preceded a German attack. U.S. 2nd Inf Div was also on the offensive: on December 11 it had been ordered to attack and seize the Roer River dams. The German assault put paid to that mission, and the division moved back to Elsenborn. As the accompanying maps show, the Elsenborn Ridge came under sustained attack for some ten days, first by 12th and 277th Volksgrenadier Divisions, who were joined by the 12th SS-Panzer Division, and finally by 3rd Panzergrenadier Division (who took over from *Hitlerjugend* when it moved south) and 246th VG Division. Reinforced by the veteran 1st Inf Div and 613th TD Battalion, the defense held firm, even when bombarded from December 21 by Werfers and attacked by 25th PzGr Regt and *Hitlerjugend*. The artillery made the difference. On the 20th 3rd PzGr Division was caught by artillery fire and its attack broken up. Then, the "1st Division Artillery, the 406th FA Group, and reinforcing batteries from the 2nd and 99th Divisions fired over 10,000 rounds in support of the Dom Bütgenbach defenders ... on the 21st." After that 12th VG Division refused to attack again without armor support. The Northern Shoulder was jammed tight.

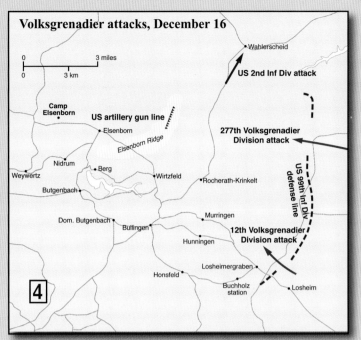

Volksgrenadier attacks, December 16

4

Map showing: Wahlerscheid, US 2nd Inf Div attack, Camp Elsenborn, US artillery gun line, Elsenborn, Elsenborn Ridge, Nidrum, Berg, Weywertz, Wirtzfeld, Rocherath-Krinkelt, 277th Volksgrenadier Division attack, Butgenbach, Dom. Butgenbach, Bullingen, Murringen, US 99th Inf Div defense line, Hunningen, 12th Volksgrenadier Division attack, Honsfeld, Losheimergraben, Losheim, Buchholz station. Scale: 0–3 miles, 0–3 km.

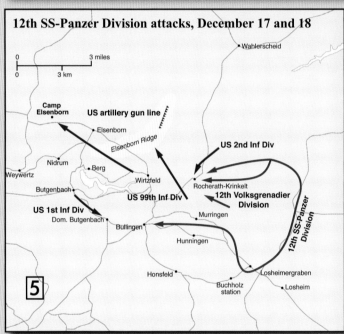

12th SS-Panzer Division attacks, December 17 and 18

5

Map showing: Wahlerscheid, Camp Elsenborn, US artillery gun line, Elsenborn, Elsenborn Ridge, US 2nd Inf Div, Nidrum, Berg, Weywertz, Wirtzfeld, Rocherath-Krinkelt, 12th Volksgrenadier Division, US 99th Inf Div, 12th SS-Panzer Division, Butgenbach, US 1st Inf Div, Dom. Butgenbach, Bullingen, Murringen, Hunningen, Honsfeld, Losheimergraben, Buchholz station, Losheim. Scale: 0–3 miles, 0–3 km.

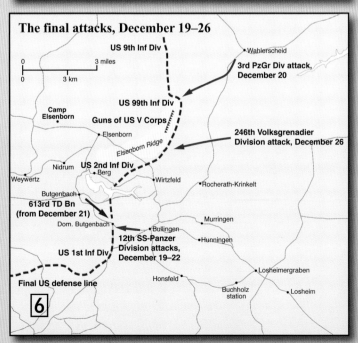

The final attacks, December 19–26

6

Map showing: US 9th Inf Div, Wahlerscheid, 3rd PzGr Div attack, December 20, US 99th Inf Div, Camp Elsenborn, Guns of US V Corps, Elsenborn, 246th Volksgrenadier Division attack, December 26, Elsenborn Ridge, Nidrum, US 2nd Inf Div, Berg, Weywertz, Wirtzfeld, Rocherath-Krinkelt, Butgenbach, 613rd TD Bn (from December 21), Dom. Butgenbach, Bullingen, Murringen, US 1st Inf Div, 12th SS-Panzer Division attacks, December 19–22, Hunningen, Honsfeld, Final US defense line, Losheimergraben, Buchholz station, Losheim. Scale: 0–3 miles, 0–3 km.

7

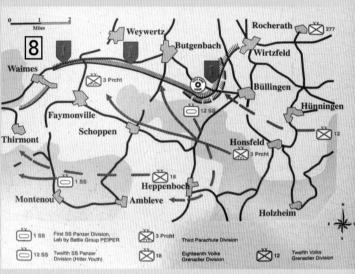

8

Map showing: Rocherath, Weywertz, Butgenboch, Wirtzfeld, Waimes, 3 Prcht, Büllingen, Faymonville, Hünningen, Schoppen, Honsfeld, 3 Prcht, 12 SS, Thirmont, 12, Montenou, 1 SS, Heppenboch, 18, Ambleve, Holzheim. Legend: 1 SS First SS Panzer Division, led by Battle Group PEIPER; 12 SS Twelfth SS Panzer Division (Hitler Youth); 3 Prcht Third Parachute Division; 18 Eighteenth Volks Grenadier Division; 12 Twelfth Volks Grenadier Division. Scale: 0–2 Miles.

9

10

Leibstandarte's Initial Advance

Below: *1 KG Peiper leaves assembly area in Blankenheim Forest; 2 Crosses the Scheid railroad bridge; 3 Büllingen fuel dump; 4 Massacre at Baugnez crossroads takes place around 14:30; 5 Peiper just misses Brig. Timberlake; 6 Stavelot bridge crossed—retaken by U.S. forces, fighting continues until December 25; 7 Wanne is taken and Mohnke moves Div HQ here on the 19th; 8 Bridges blown at Trois-Ponts (Amblève 11:15; Salm 13:00); 9 Cheneux bridge found intact, air attack c. 14:30; 10 Peiper is stymied at Neufmoulin; 11 Returns to La Gleize where elements of KG Knittel join; 12 Attack though Stoumont and Târgnon held at Stoumont Station; 13 Denouement at La Gleize; 14 Retreat by 800 survivors to Wanne; 15 Petit Spai bridge where the last LSSAH troops north of the Amblève crossed back on Dec 25.*

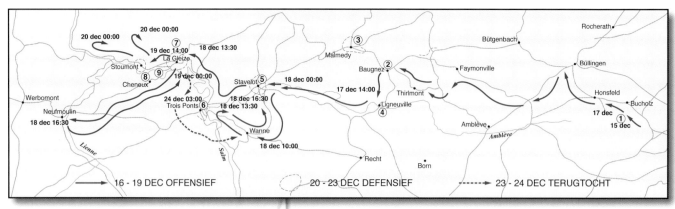

Top and Below: *99th Inf Div POWs make their way through Merlscheid (top) and a King Tiger of 501st SS-sPzAbt passes the same POWs as it motors towards Lanzerath. German infantry quickly rounded up about 300 prisoners in Honsfeld and some 200 more at Büllingen.*

Opposite: *As one drives along the narrow roads past Merlscheid church, it's easy to envisage the length of the Leibstandarte column—and the easy pickings for U.S. fighter-bombers when they got airborne. Opposite Merlscheid church this M5 3-inch ATk gun speaks of another holdup to the Leibstandarte advance. Today the farmhouse has seen additions.*

3 Fifth Panzerarmee

M4A3 (76mm) of Coy B, 2nd Tank Bn,
U.S. 9th Armd Div (see pp. 52–53).

Above: *All quiet in St. Vith in September, two months before the offensive, as a 7th Armd Div halftrack negotiates the winding streets.*

Below: *The northern part of Hasso von Manteuffel's Fifth Panzerarmee's attack, December 16–19, towards St. Vith. Held up by valiant 28th Infantry defense, the timetable of the attack was knocked out of kilter. A number of 28th Infantry units retreated to Bastogne and played an important part in the defense.*

Opposite, Above Right: *CCB of 9th Armd Div was commanded by Brig William M. Hoge. It had been attached to 2nd Inf Div pending the attack on the Roer River dams, but on December 16 started a week of continuous action defending the approaches to St. Vith and later the town itself.*

Opposite, Below: *Whereas Sixth SS-Panzerarmee had six Rollbahnen, Manteuffel had two, the upper (used by LVIII Panzerkorps (spearheaded by 116th Pz Div) towards Houffalize, La Roche, and Namur. The other used by XLVII Panzerkorps (2nd Pz Div and Panzer Lehr) headed for Bastogne and then on towards Dinant and Givet.*

I n his definitive official history of the Battle of the Bulge, Hugh M. Cole talks about "Cannae in the Schnee Eifel" referring back to Hannibal's brilliant double-encirclement of the Roman Army on August 2, 216 BC. It may be overstating the size of the victory won by LXVI Korps (under General der Artillerie Walter Lucht) of von Manteuffel's Fifth Panzerarmee as it encircled the U.S. forces on the Schnee Eifel—primarily the 106th Inf Div—but by forcing the surrender of the 422nd and 423rd Infantry regiments on December 19, upward of 7,000 entered captivity. This was a dark day for the U.S. Army, its only significant defeat in the ETO from Normandy to Berlin. It was gained by two Volksgrenadier divisions (18th and 62nd) who would be joined in their attack on the next objective, St. Vith, but the Führer Begleit Brigade. The remnants of the 106th retreated to St. Vith and the battle for the town was intense, crucially delaying the German attack, and is covered separately in Chapter 7.

The southern sector of the Fifth Panzerarmee's front saw 28th Inf Div attacked by LVIII and XLVII Panzerkorps, which included armored thrusts by the 116th and 2nd Pz Divs and Panzer Lehr. The 116th Pz Div reached Houffalize on December 19 before striking north to take Samrée, Dochamps, and Verdenne by Christmas Eve. However, dogged defense slowed up the German advance and by the time the 28th was withdrawn for reorganization on December 22, it had won time to allow Bastogne to be reinforced by Brig Gen McAuliffe and the 101st Airborne along with elements of the 10th Armd Div, of which more later.

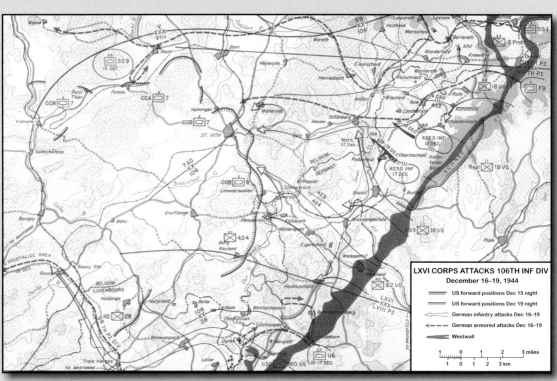

LXVI CORPS ATTACKS 106TH INF DIV
December 16–19, 1944

US forward positions Dec 15 night
US forward positions Dec 19 night
German infantry attacks Dec 16–19
German armored attacks Dec 16–19
Westwall

1Lt Eric Fisher Wood

Above Meyerode stands a tribute to "Capt" (actually Lt) Eric Wood, of Bty A, 589th FA Bn, 106th Inf Div. His unit was caught up in the fighting around Auw and on December 17 retreated to Schönberg on the Our. There his unit was ambushed and many were taken prisoner, but Wood escaped into the trees. The next day, near Meyerode, Peter Maraite met Wood and another American soldier, and took them home. Over a meal Wood told him that he was going to make for St. Vith or start his own private war. Over the next few days Maraite heard gunfire and Sepp Dietrich, whose HQ was in the village, complained about "scoundrels and bandits" harassing troops in the woods. When the village was liberated on January 23, 1945, the frozen body of an American soldier was found in the woods a mile south. In May that year, the Maraite family was visited by Gen Eric Fisher Wood, SR and the identity of the soldier was confirmed. There's a great deal of speculation and rumor about what happened in the woods—much of it prompted by the general who wanted to honor his son. There's no corroboration of many of the Hollywood-style stories that have been proposed in books and articles about Eric Fisher Wood's "private war": whether he was alone or not; whether 200 graves of German soldiers were found in the woods or not; exactly when Wood died; and who his companion was. In the end, Eric Fisher Wood was awarded the DSC and the citation says, "he repeatedly initiated ambush attacks against enemy communications, supply columns, and patrols, accounting for the deaths of scores of the foe."

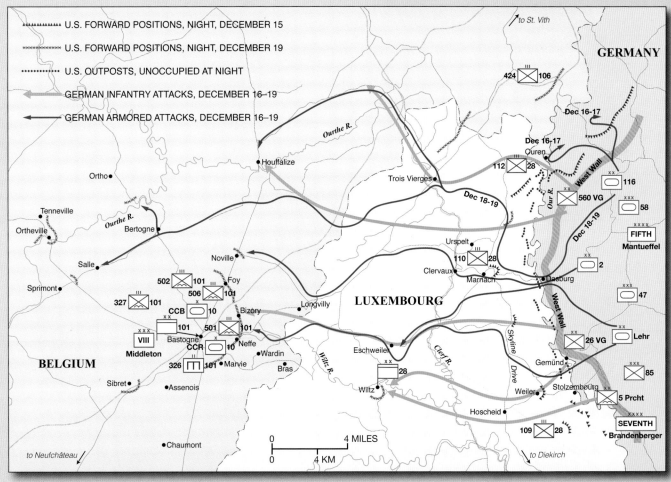

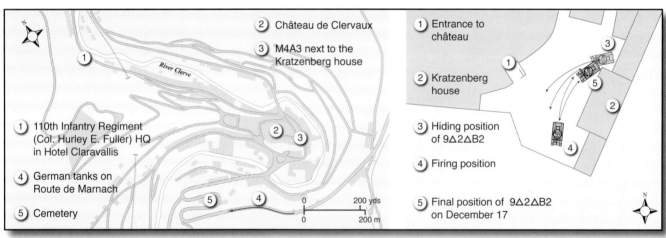

① 110th Infantry Regiment (Col. Hurley E. Fuller) HQ in Hotel Claravallis

② Château de Clervaux

③ M4A3 next to the Kratzenberg house

④ German tanks on Route de Marnach

⑤ Cemetery

River Clerve

0 ___ 200 yds
0 ___ 200 m

① Entrance to château

② Kratzenberg house

③ Hiding position of 9△2△B2

④ Firing position

⑤ Final position of 9△2△B2 on December 17

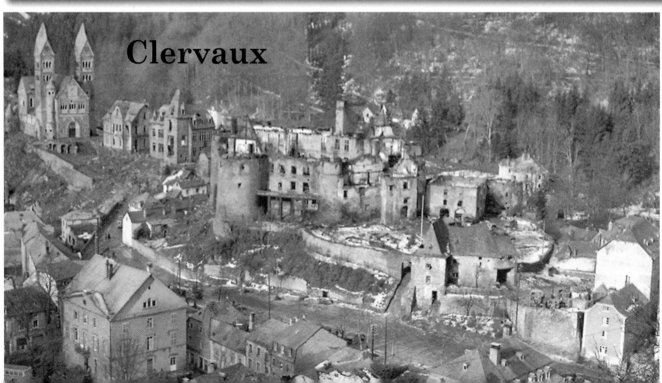

Clervaux

Opposite: *Clervaux (Clerf in German) stood directly on the XLVII Panzerkorps route towards Bastogne on the lower of Fifth Panzerarmee's Rollbahnen. During the battle with 2nd Pz Div, a handful of 28th Inf Div soldiers, led by Capt John Aitken, were besieged on December 17—the so-called "Luxembourg Alamo." Outside are a number of guns and an M4A3 (76mm) of Coy B, 2nd Tank Bn, 9th Armd Div (as illustrated on pp. 48–49), one of five tanks which supported the 28th Inf Div. This one fired at Germans on the Marnach road, retreating behind cover after he had done so. Hit twice but still functioning, the tank was abandoned after it reversed into the house it was using as cover. Subsequently another German round pierced the turret. Past and present views of the city show the medieval castle (XIIth century) and the deanship's church (1910–1912). Destroyed during the Battle of Clervaux, after the war the burnt-out castle ruins were restored. Part now houses the Museum of the Battle of the Bulge. (Drawings based on those from Diorama-Clervaux.) Jean-Pol Grandmont/ WikiCommons (top photo)*

Above Left: *Clervaux boasts the CEBA's Memorial to the American infantryman.*

Above: *This PaK 43/41 (88mm) is in the castle grounds. The most powerful German antitank gun, Krupp's PaK 43 was produced in two versions—the 43 had a cruciform mount; the 43/41 used the two-wheel split-trail carriage (as here) from the 10cm leichte Kanone 41. A version of this gun armed the Tiger II.*

Center Left and Left: *Knocked out opponents in Clervaux. The cemetery is on the zigzags of the Marnach road.*

Houffalize

Below Right: *Kampfgruppe Stephan of 116th Pz Div was commanded by Maj Eberhard Stephan. At Marnach it defeated 707th TD Bn's D Co, before taking Troisvierges after a fight on December 18. This is a PaK 43 88mm—on a cruciform mount (cf the 43/41 on the previous page).*

Bottom Right: *The bad weather meant that the Allies were unable to call on close support aircraft, but equally important was the absence of PR material. When the weather cleared, PR resumed immediately and this photo shows graphically how useful it was. This is Mont, just north of Houffalize, on December 26, as taken by 16th PR Sqn, RAF— part of the Strategic Reconnaissance Wing of the 2TAF. A high-altitude PR squadron, it was based at RAF Blackbushe and equipped with Spitfire PR Mk XIs which could, in an emergency, climb to 44,000ft (13,000m). It could carry vertically mounted cameras behind the cockpit or vertically oriented cameras under the wings.*

Opposite: *Houffalize was taken by 116th Panzer Division on December 19 but this Panther G, original turret number 111 now marked 401, probably from I./16th Pz Regt, was knocked out later as the First and Third Armies fought to reduce the "Bulge." Local accounts suggest it was toppled into the river because of bombing and that the crew died as a result. The Panther was recovered from the Ourthe by engineers on September 20, 1948, and has been moved up the hill to become a memorial, as the modern photos show. Houffalize was badly damaged during the fighting and a replacement bridge was needed over the River Ourthe. To block the transit of German supplies—and the possible use of the roads as an escape route for German forces—ninety RAF Lancasters bombed the town on the night of January 5–6, 1945.*

Houffalize, like Bastogne, Vielsalm, and St. Vith, was a crucial crossroads and river-crossing in the central Ardennes. It was taken without a fight on December 19, as LVIII Panzerkorps—spearheaded by 116th Pz Division—advanced from Ouren and Troisvierges. From Houffalize the Panzerkorps headed towards Namur but was unable to maintain its initial momentum, mainly because of the same issues that dogged all the German thrusts: lack of fuel, problems with bridges, and stubborn defense. Advancing initially from Houffalize towards Bertogne, with doubts about available bridges over the Ourthe, Gen. Walter Krüger decide to backtrack through Houffalize along the other side of the river towards Samrée and Dochamps. On the 20th, when they reached Samrée, they captured fuel and rations—it was a 7th Armd Div main depot—and then moved on to take Dochamps. Their lead Kampfgruppe, KG Bayer (under Oberst Johannes Bayer),, moved north to Beffe and came into contact with the task forces of newly arrived 3rd Armd Div. (The story continues in Chapter 11.)

4 Attack in the South

This Page: *Vianden Castle was the scene of a remarkable battle on November 19,1944, before the Ardennes offensive when members of the Luxembourg Resistance fought off 250 soldiers of the Waffen-SS. A month later, and the Germans were back. This time, the ruins of Vianden Castle were held by 2/109th Infantry of 28th Division. After an initial bombardment, 5th FJR Division made their away across the Our and took the castle and town. Postwar the castle was completely restored to a state it had not enjoyed since the 18th century.*

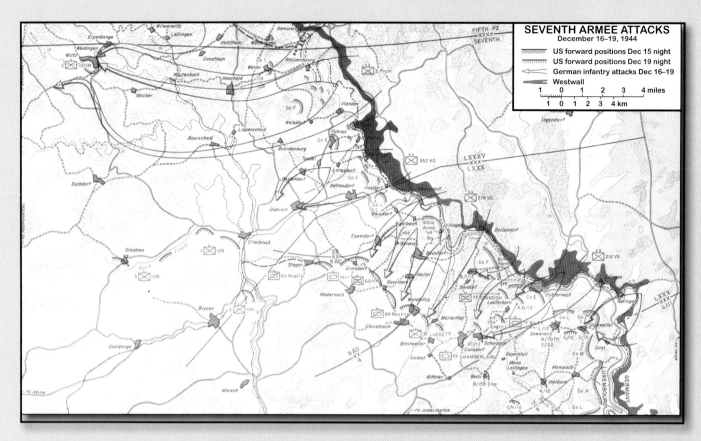

SEVENTH ARMEE ATTACKS
December 16–19, 1944

///////// US forward positions Dec 15 night
⊓⊓⊓⊓⊓⊓ US forward positions Dec 19 night
◄─── German infantry attacks Dec 16–19
▬▬◄ Westwall

1 0 1 2 3 4 miles
1 0 1 2 3 4 km

Above: *The advances of Seventh Armee December 16–19. In the north, alongside the Fifth Panzerarmee advance, the Fallschirmjäger played a major role in taking Wiltz. In the process the 110th Regiment of 28th Division was badly mauled. In the south the 109th Regiment fared better and the German inroads were kept to about four miles' depth. Counterattacks on December 21–26 pushed the Germans back to the Sauer, although they held Diekirch.*

Below Right and Opposite: *Esch-sur-Sûre is a pretty town on a oxbow bend of the river that played an important role in the Allied counterattack, when the destroyed bridge over the Sûre was replaced on December 27. The classic photo of the Beutepanzer—in German nomenclature PzKpfw M4 748 (a)—highlights a German asset and problem in one. Controlling Europe for three years allowed them to pillage the manufacturing capability of many countries and appropriate many weapons. They put them to good use—but this meant ammunition came in hundreds of different forms and made resupply a nightmare.*

Brandenberger's Seventh Armee was tasked with the provision of flank defense for Fifth Panzerarmee. Infantry heavy, it had no tanks and only thirty assault guns; little bridging equipment and a number of rivers to cross. The area it attacked was defended by the 109th Inf Regt (commanded by Lt Col James Rudder of Rangers fame) of the 28th Inf Div, under another D-Day hero, Brig. Norman Cota and, to the south, another D-Day connection—4th Inf Div under Maj Gen "Tubby" Barton, both divisions trying to bed in replacements for the casualties of the battle of the Hürtgen Forest. Between these infantry divisions was 60th AIB of 9th Armd Div.

In the north, alongside Fifth Panzerarmee, 5th FJR Division advanced and took Wiltz on December 19. Further south, however, progress was slow. Although the attack made immediate gains and advanced some four to five miles taking Echternach, Berdorf, and Diekirch, the American forces gave up ground slowly, using their artillery effectively, denying the enemy opportunities to build bridges over the Sauer. The limited U.S. armor assets also proved their worth. U.S. casualties were high—some 2,000 between December 16 and 21—but the Germans lost more and the attack petered out.

The critical battles were about to start, but they wouldn't happen on the southern shoulder, where counterattacks by 4th Inf Div and 10th Armd Div pushed the German forces back to the Sauer. The southern shoulder, in Cole's words, was "jammed."

Above: *Wiltz was the command post of 28th Inf Div from December 19. The division played a valiant role in holding off the German attacks towards Bastogne. Hugh Cole sums it up, "The fall of Wiltz ended the 28th Division's delaying action before Bastogne ... without the gallant bargain struck by the 110th Infantry and its Allied units—men for time—the German plans for a coup-de-main at Bastogne would have turned to accomplished fact."*

Right: *28th Cav Recon Sqn in Wiltz in January 1945.*

Opposite:
1 *Soldiers from the 28th Division in Wiltz on December 20.*

2 *Memorial "To the 28th U.S. Infantry Division which liberated Wiltz on Sept 10th 1944 and gallantly defended our soil during the Battle of the Bulge."*

3 *Members of B/630th TD Bn, who lost their vehicles during advancement to Belgium, take infantry positions on a hill covering an approach to Wiltz, on December 20.*

4–6 *Memorials to: Eisenhower who visited Wiltz when it was HQ 28th Division before the Battle of the Bulge (4); various divisions including the 4th at Osweiler (5); 10th Armd Div at Berdorf (6).*

Wiltz

Right: *Diekirch was liberated on September 11, 1944 by units of the U.S. 5th Armd Div. The 109th moved into Diekirch at the beginning of December 1944. The 2nd and 3rd Bns were assigned to the front line, with the 1st Bn in reserve in Diekirch; the regimental HQ was at Ettelbrück. The 109th was backed up by the 107th (105mm) and 108th (155 mm) FA Bns from high ground north of Diekirch, and had Sherman tanks of the 707th Tank Bn attached. In case of emergency, nearby was 3rd FA Bn of CCA, 9th Armd Div, as well as other units of the 28th Inf Div. The 3rd Bn was attacked by the 915th and 916th Regiments of the 352nd VG Division; the 2nd Bn was attacked by the 914th Regt and units of 5th FJR Division, who took Fouhren. As the Germans finally bridged the Sauer, the U.S. forces moved back, and finally had to leave Diekirch—the civilian evacuation following on from the military withdrawal on December 20. The German advance continued until it hit Third Army's 80th Inf Div. The Germans were forced back: Ettelbrück was liberated on December 23 but Diekirch would have to wait until January 21, 1945, to be liberated again by U.S. 5th Inf Div.*

Diekirch

Below: *M4A1(76)W HVSS is in the grounds of the Musée National d'Histoire Militaire, in Diekirch. This improved version of the M4 medium didn't reach Europe until the end of the war and wouldn't have seen action during the Battle of the Bulge.*

9th ARMORED DIVISION

This 1985 memorial in Medernach commemorates the exploits of 9th Armd Div (Maj Gen. John W. Leonard) in defense of Luxembourg Oct 20–Dec 26, 1944 and Belgium Dec 16, 1944–Jan 4, 1945. The division's three combat commands fought the Ardennes battle as independent, widely separated units attached to other divisions and corps on the north, center, and south of the German attack, as described on the plaques. Hastily organized forces composed of cooks, clerks, mechanics, and others from the headquarters of divisional units defended the Berg-Mersch area from Dec 16 to 23, and then established a counter-reconnaissance screen extending 50 kilometers northwest from Neufchateau, Belgium. Peter Valstar via STIWOT

CCB

Reaching St. Vith on December 17, after a forced march from Faymonville, CCB repulsed German attacks from the northeast and the southeast. After the arrival of other U.S. forces it skillfully and valiantly defended the southern sector of the St. Vith redoubt until ordered to Werbomont. Arriving on December 25, by delaying the German advance during the critical early days of the Ardennes Offensive, CCB contributed significantly to the failure of the German attack in the northern sector, for which it was cited in the Order of the Day of the Belgian Army.

For extraordinary heroism and gallantry in combat in Belgium from December 17 to 23, 1944, CCB was awarded the U.S. Presidential Unit Citation on June 12, 2001.

CCA

By stopping the German attack of Dec 16, 1944, at the Ermsdorf–Waldbillig line, CCA saved the farms and towns in the Medernach–Larochette area and gained that vital time and space needed to launch the American attack to lift besieged Bastogne. Relieved on December 26, CCA marched all that night to Neufchateau, broke through and dispersed German forces blocking the highway to Bastogne and then continued attacking west of Bastogne until relieved on January 4, 1945. For extraordinary heroism and gallantry in combat in Luxembourg from December 16 to 22, 1944, CCA was awarded the U.S. Presidential Unit Citation on June 12, 2001.

CCR

From Dec 16 to 19, CCR defended roadblocks on the Troisvierges–Bastogne highway against German Panzer and infantry divisions. Surrounded and decimated near Longvilly, its survivors reached Bastogne where, as the nucleus of famed "Team Snafu" they joined in its defense until relieved on Dec 31. By delaying the German advance during the critical early days of the Ardennes Offensive, CCR gained the time needed for other U.S. units to concentrate at, and hold, Bastogne, for which it was awarded the U.S. Presidential Unit Citation (Army) and the Belgian Croix De Guerre with Palm.

Memorial at Marnach. On the left, a plaque devoted to 707th Tank Battalion (detail above right) and on the right: "In honor to the 28th U.S. Infantry 'Keystone' Division Liberator and Defender of Marnach 1944" (below right).

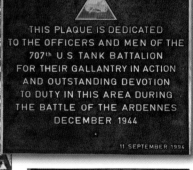

THIS PLAQUE IS DEDICATED TO THE OFFICERS AND MEN OF THE 707th U.S TANK BATTALION FOR THEIR GALLANTRY IN ACTION AND OUTSTANDING DEVOTION TO DUTY IN THIS AREA DURING THE BATTLE OF THE ARDENNES DECEMBER 1944

11 SEPTEMBER 1994

IN HONOR TO THE 28th U.S. INFANTRY "KEYSTONE" DIVISION LIBERATOR AND DEFENDER OF MARNACH 1944

ERIGE PAR LA COMMUNE DE MUNSHAUSEN 1989 150e ANNIVERSAIRE DE L'INDEPENDANCE DU GRAND DUCHE DE LUXEMBOURG

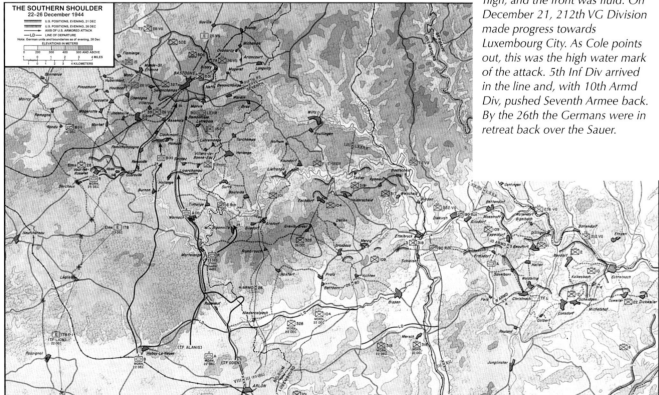

6

Opposite: *Memorials to those who fought in Luxembourg in 1944–45.*
1 *At Dahl to 80th Inf Div soldiers killed in this area in January 1945. It also commemorates the killed or missing residents of the town.*

2 *At Hosingen (Housen), three stones, each with a plaque to those who helped in the defense and liberation of the town: the paratroopers of the U.S. 17th AB Division for the liberation in 1945; K Coy, 110th Infantry and B Coy 103rd ECB both of 28th Inf Div for their defense of the town; and to Ralph R. Wardle and John W. Kelly of D Coy, 702nd Tank Bn, who died on January 27, 1945.*

3 *Memorial to I Coy, 110th Regiment, 28th Inf Div, who fought in Weiler in December 1944.*

4 *The National Liberation Memorial at Schumann's Eck includes a memorial to the units that fought in the area—28th, 26th, 90th Inf Divs and 6th U.S. Cav Group (Mecz).*

5 and 6 *These photos show men of 5th Inf Div in Luxembourg on December 29.*

Below: *The attack on U.S. 4th Inf Div positions had the benefit of surprise, but tenacious defense and excellent artillery work, along with support from 10th Armd Div, ensured that little ground was given up. Casualties were high, and the front was fluid. On December 21, 212th VG Division made progress towards Luxembourg City. As Cole points out, this was the high water mark of the attack. 5th Inf Div arrived in the line and, with 10th Armd Div, pushed Seventh Armee back. By the 26th the Germans were in retreat back over the Sauer.*

THE SOUTHERN SHOULDER
22–26 December 1944

5 The Allies' Reaction

As might be expected, the events of December 16 brought a quick reaction from the Allied high command. Even though no one was immediately sure about the scale or nature of the attack, 12th Army Group commander Omar N. Bradley was with Supreme Commander Dwight D. Eisenhower in Versailles, just outside Paris, celebrating Ike's fifth star, and they discussed the immediate reaction. Bradley thought it "a spoiling attack" to disrupt First Army's attack on the Roer River dams. Ike suggested that 7th Armd Div should move into the area from Ninth Army in the north and 10th Armd Div from Third Army in the south. Patton wasn't happy: he was expecting to launch an attack himself, but freed the division to move to Middleton's VIII Corps from December 17. To stop any further units being taken, Patton urged Gen Manton Eddy to get 4th Armd Div into the attack quickly, but later on the 17th, presciently suggested that Third Army would have to move north to save the day and discussed such a move with III Corps' CG, Maj Gen John Millikin.

A little further down the pecking order, Hodges and Simpson of First and Ninth armies respectively discussed further reinforcements. In consequence of this, 1st Inf Div's 26th Regiment moved to Camp Elsenborn (arriving 07:00 on the 17th). Just before 12:00 on the 17th Leland S. Hobbs, CG of 30th Inf Div, was told to move south to block any move against Liège. And when Bradley got back to Luxembourg City from Versailles, Hodges called him requesting the two airborne divisions in reserve in France: the 82nd and 101st. Ike finally agreed to this at 19:00 and they were ordered to Bastogne. However, Hodges then proposed one to Bastogne and one to Werbomont. Initially it was the 82nd that was chosen for Bastogne with 101st heading for Werbomont. As it happened, by the time 82nd was en route to Bastogne, Hodges' concerns about KG Peiper led to that division being ordered to Werbomont.

With the Germans hot-footing it towards Bastogne, Troy Middleton, commander of VIII Corps, amended the orders to 10th Armd Div, sending its leading combat command to Bastogne, while other elements of the

division dug in to protect Luxembourg City. Middleton moved his HQ out of Bastogne to Neufchateau but with great coolness waited for Col Roberts, CCB 10th Armd Div's CO, to arrive before leaving himself. He ordered Roberts to send teams to Noville (Team Desobry), the Ettelbrück road (Team O'Hara), and Longvilly (Team Cherry). Middleton also briefed Brig Gen Anthony C. McAuliffe, acting commander of 101st AB Division, whose men started to arrive in Bastogne around midnight on December 18. They had won the race for Bastogne because of the staunch defense by 28th Inf Division—the Germans arrived in strength the next day. Charles B. MacDonald says baldly: "Had the 2nd Panzer Division and 26th VG Division crossed the Clerve River on the first day, December 16, the Germans would have captured Bastogne, and the Panzer Lehr Division would have been free to join 2nd Panzer Division in a drive to the Meuse." It was the men of 110th Infantry from 28th Division and 10th Armd Div's Team Cherry who won the day.

On December 18, Patton met Bradley in Luxembourg City. Apprised of the facts, Patton changed his position. Far from pushing on with his attack in the south he said he could get 4th Armored and 80th Infantry divisions moving north immediately, and 26th Infantry in twenty-four hours. Ordering his staff to get working on the detail, he remarked, "The Krauts have stuck their head into a meatgrinder, and I have hold of the handle." It was, therefore, unsurprising that he repeated the suggestion the next day at Verdun when he and Bradley met Eisenhower, and on getting Eisenhower's agreement, made it happen.

What was, perhaps, more surprising was Eisenhower's decision on the 20th to place FM Montgomery in charge of American forces in the north—First and Ninth armies. Much debated—particularly after an inept Press conference by Monty on January 7, 1945—it was undoubtedly the correct military decision (ask Clarke of St. Vith!), but Monty's PR debacle and seventy years of post facto vituperation have effectively obscured his cool and incisive generalship. Perhaps the last word is best left to Manteuffel whose summation of Montgomery's role was that he " turned a series of isolated actions into a coherent battle fought according to a clear and definite plan. It was his refusal to engage in premature and piecemeal counter-attacks which enabled the Americans to gather their reserves and frustrate the German attempts to extend their breakthrough."

Whatever the rights and wrongs of the command decisions, the actions taken by the senior commanders of the Allied armies between December 16 and 20 ensured that the slight glimmering of opportunity afforded to the Germans after their initial attacks succeeded would later be quashed—but it took a lot of hard fighting to make it happen.

Above: *Montgomery inspects British 6th Airborne Division. Crossing the Channel by sea, on December 26 the division was between Dinant and Namur, with the 3rd Parachute Brigade on the left, the 5th on the right, and the 6th Airlanding Brigade in reserve.*

Below: *Moving anywhere in the Ardennes was difficult in the winter of 1944. Those traveling the battlefields today must remember what seventy-five years of progress have brought us: metaled roads, municipal snowplows, gritting and other road protection. Back in 1944–45 the roads were muddy, single-track affairs that led to traffic jams of immense proportions. The unsung heroes of all armies were the men who kept the traffic moving: logistics experts, the MPs, and the engineers who mended bridges, filled craters, and bulldozed rubble*

82nd Airborne

Below, Bottom, and Below Right
Memorial to 82nd Airborne at Werbomont. In the background a British 25-pounder which has been refitted with a 105mm barrel as used postwar by the Belgian Army.

While there is no doubt that the "Battered Bastards of Bastogne" gained the headlines, the "All Americans" were responsible for defeating the most dangerous of all the German attacks: that of Sixth SS-Panzerarmee spearheaded by Jochen Peiper's Kampfgruppe of 1st SS-Panzer Division *Leibstandarte Adolf Hitler*. Alerted in their quarters at Camps Suippes and Sissonne, France, they were originally intended for Bastogne, but 82nd was redirected north to Werbomont.

In conjunction with 3rd Armd Div and engineer units from 1111th Engineer Combat Group (especially the 291st Engineer Combat Battalion), the 504th PIR attacked Peiper from December 19, outfought this heavily armed unit, and kept him deprived of fuel and reinforcements. Eventually, Peiper abandoned his armor on December 24, and he and some 800 men returned to German lines on foot.

South of the 504th, the 505th reinforced Trois-Ponts and along the Salm; the 508th moved to Vielsalm and Salmchâteau; and the 325th GIR to Barvaux, Grandmenil, Hebronval, Regne, and Fraiture.

Fifth Panzerarmee's attack progressed, reaching the isolated key road junction of Baraque de Fraiture. Gavin rushed a company of glider troops there and a glider infantry battalion to the town of Fraiture, a mile northeast of the crossroads. The two units arrived on the morning of December 22, just in time to confront 2nd SS-Panzer Division. Heavily outnumbered, the GIs at Baraque de Fraiture stood their ground for more than an hour but were overwhelmed. Only forty-four of the 116 glider troops sent to the junction escaped; the rest were killed or captured.

Meanwhile, the position of St. Vith had become untenable and on December 21, around 21:30, Brig Gen Bruce Clarke, ordered the remaining American forces to withdraw to the west. They did so, and moved back to the American lines. It was at this point that, to Gavin's dismay, Montgomery shortened the lines to improve communications and coordination. On the 24th the 82nd moved to a line Trois-Ponts, Erria, Manhay. And there they held as the final Fifth Panzerarmee attacks petered out. On January 3, the 82nd went on the offensive. Before a week passed, they had regained the ground they had lost, in the process destroying the 62nd VG Division. 82nd was relieved on January 10.

Above Left and Above: *Memorial to 82nd Airborne at Rochinval: "110 paratroopers retook this town on 3-1-1945 there were 790 in 4 days of fighting 680 including their Commander Lt Col Wood G. Joerg fell on the battlefield Rochinval."*

Left: *Troopers of the 504th PIR pass a 57mm AT gun of the 80th AB AA Bn, as they enter Cheneux.*

Below Left: *Men of the 325th GIR drag a heavily loaded ammunition sled through the snow, near Herresbach, Belgium on January 28. They had a few days out of combat before spearheading the attack NE of St. Vith and then against the Siegfried Line.*

Below: *Maj Gen James Gavin negotiates a well-trodden path in Belgium during the beginning phases of the Battle of the Bulge. He's carrying his signature M1 Garand rifle.*

101st Airborne

When orders to move towards Bastogne went out to the 101st Airborne it was resting near Reims, France. After Market Garden the 82nd had been pulled out of Holland first and was on the road first, taking trucks past Bastogne to Werbomont, farther north. Assembling the 101st was easier said than done since the Screaming Eagles had been out of the line for less than a month and had turned over most of their weapons. Officer teams had to scour Paris to fetch in men on leave. By the 18th enough vehicles (mainly open-air cattle trucks) had been assembled and the division took to the road, many of the paratroopers without guns or ammo. During the dark, early morning hours of December 19 the 101st Airborne arrived at Bastogne.

The paratroopers' advance toward forward positions was impeded by a flood of retreating, often panicked, troops heading the other way, though this allowed the troopers to cadge weapons and ammo on their march. At Noville the 10th Armd Div's TF Desobry lost half its vehicles and the paratroopers fell back to Foy. At nearby Longvilly, the 10th CCB's Task Force Cherry, along with the HQ of the 9th's CCR, was overrun. On the 21st the Panzer Lehr Division circuited Bastogne from the south, cutting off its contact with the rest of the U.S. front, while the 26th Volksgrenadier Division filled in the ring. By December 23, even as Panzer spearheads drove on for the Meuse, elements of nine German divisions surrounded Bastogne. Paratroopers of the 101st Division, manning lonely foxholes in woods and fields on the town's periphery, fought off German assaults by day and endured artillery barrages at night. Hitler switched the entire focus of the offensive to the south, which meant that the bleeding sore of Bastogne had to be eliminated. It became a race to see who could get there first: Patton's reinforcing Third Army or a new flood of SS troops pouring down from the north.

Elements of Third Army won the race. They met the 326th Engineers at around 16:50 on December 26. A day later Lt Maxwell D. Taylor reached Bastogne with the 4th Armd Div and resumed command of the 101st Airborne. The battle didn't stop there: immediately after the siege had been lifted, Third Army fought to widen the narrow corridor to Bastogne before moving on northward to crush the remnants of the attacking force. In early January the Allies attacked the "Bulge." It was slow progress, but Patton, as aggressive as ever, pushed on—with the 101st leading the way—first to a meeting with First Army at Houffalize in mid-January and then toward the Siegfried Line. The "Bulge" ceased to exist on January 25.

Above: *America's most famous unit of WW2? In 2002 veterans of 101st's E Co, 506th PIR—the "Band of Brothers"—planted a tree as a memorial to their action at Rachamps. BoomBoomBeem/ WikiCommons CC BY-SA 3.0*

Below: *Men of the 101st Airborne move out of Bastogne on December 29.*

Above Left: *A new monument was unveiled at Sainte-Ode, Luxembourg on the 65th anniversary of the Battle of the Bulge for the 326th Airborne Medical Company, 101st Airborne Division. The unit came under attack on Dec. 19, 1944. Those who survived were taken as prisoners of war, until the end of the war. "In the field behind this monument the Division Clearing Station of the 326th Airborne Medical Company was overrun by enemy forces. On the night of December 19, 1944, enemy forces attacked with armored vehicles and infantry. The hospital was sprayed by machine-gun fire for a period of fifteen minutes and many soldiers were killed or wounded. Those who survived this attack became prisoners of war. This site is to memorize all the victims and to honor the 326th Airborne Medical Company and all other medical units who served during WW2. They had their rendezvous with destiny. May this monument be a symbol of honor for those brave men and women who were willing to give their lives while saving others, some came home but so many didn't. MAY THE WORLD NEVER FORGET." Ms. Christie Vanover (IMCOM)*

Above: *101st Airborne roadblock on the Bastogne preimeter.*

Center Left: *Soldiers from the 101st move north, December 19. Note 2.36-inch bazooka crew. These teams would prove their worth over the days ahead with many successes—such as John Ballard who accounted for one of the two tanks destroyed by paratroopers around Champs on Christmas morning. But the U.S. Army bazooka wasn't the best. Gen. James M. Gavin said the 82nd "did not get adequate antitank weapons until it began to capture the first German Panzerfausts. By fall '44 we had truckloads of them ... They were the best hand-carried antitank weapon of the war."*

Left: *1/506th PIR heads out to Noville to support Team Desobry who were hard pressed by 2nd Panzer Division, December 19.*

30th Infantry

At rest after heavy fighting during the battle of Aachen and during the Roer River battles at Geilenkirchen, Warden, and Lohn in October and November, 30th Infantry was in reserve when the Germans attacked. First Army's CG, Courtney Hodges, contacted Ninth Army's Bill Simpson and asked for "Old Hickory" to help. Simpson—who had commanded the division earlier in the war—had known Hodges since fighting together in World War I and immediately sent the division south. It moved through Malmédy on December 18—hitherto the town had been occupied by the 291st Engineer Combat Battalion—and westwards, taking Stavelot. During the fighting oon the western outskirts of Malmédy, one of the division, Pfc Francis S. Currey, won the Congressional Medal of Honor. Another of the division's men, T/Sgt Paul Bolden, earned the Congressional Medal of Honor in an action at Petit-Coo, on the Stoumont road out of Trois-Ponts.

The battle for Stavelot was hard and the 30th Division held it against counterattacks by elements of 1st SS-Panzer Division *Leibstandarte*—both KG Peiper attacking to open the way for resupplies and reinforcements, and the other *Kampfgruppen* as they tried to fight their way through to Peiper. After Peiper's assault concluded at La Gleize, 30th Infantry cleared KG Knittel from the banks of the Amblève, before being involved with the Allied counterattack towards St. Vith.

Below: *Elements of U.S. 30th Inf Div guard a demolition-prepared bridge in Malmédy, December 22. The city was bombed repeatedly by the USAAF over the next three nights, killing some 200 civilians.*

Bottom: *Private Gene Heathcote directs traffic direction as the 30th Inf Div moves through Malmédy after a snowfall.*

Above: *Soldiers of the 30th Inf Div in Malmédy, December 29. After spearheading the breakout from Normandy, 30th Inf Div was at Mortain when the Germans counterattacked. There, for the first time, they came into contact with 1st SS-Panzer Division and gave it a bloody nose, earning the title "Roosevelt's SS" from propagandist Axis Sally.*

Left and Below: *The 30th Inf Div HQ in Malmédy—the trees showing seventy-five years of growth.*

Today, La Gleize is a site of pilgrimage for armor fans as it boasts the only Tiger II visible to the public from the roadside, one of only seven survivors of the 489 built. 213 was disabled while sited near Wérimont Farm, to the south of the village.

Top and Above: *This well-known photo shows Luftwaffe troops changing footwear at the crossroads in Honsfeld on the way to Büllingen. Today, there's a memorial to the 612th and 801st TD Bns attached to 99th Inf Div (above).*

Above Right and Right: *An SdKfz 251 moves through Honsfeld towards Büllingen. The village was an R&R area for 99th Inf Div—Marlene Dietrich was expected to perform here on December 17 after having played Diekirch on the 16th—and many were asleep when Leibstandarte attacked. Today the crossroads is little changed save for the memorial.*

1st SS-Panzer Division *Leibstandarte Adolf Hitler* was chosen to lead the Sixth Army attack and the spearhead of that division was Kampfgruppe Peiper. After all its struggles in Russia and Normandy, the *Leibstandarte*—now fully re-equipped and rested—was eager to prove itself again.

Infantry units were designated to attack first, to open the way for the panzer divisions, but they encountered surprisingly dogged resistance from the U.S. 99th Inf Div, and by midafternoon a path for the panzers had not been cleared. Peiper, growing increasingly frustrated at the delay, just bulled his column through and reached Lanzerath by 22:00.

On December 17, Peiper's column was on the move by 03:30, mopping up isolated U.S. units on the way. It was still dark when they reached the village of Honsfeld, and the Germans were surprised to see U.S. military vehicles parked on all the streets, and most of the soldiers asleep in the houses. From here Peiper diverted to Büllingen, on *Hitlerjugend*'s route because he had heard of a U.S. fuel dump there. Should he have attacked north, toward Wirtzfeld where he could have overrun the HQ of the U.S. 2nd Division, and opened the way for the *Hitlerjugend*? He didn't, getting back to his own Rollbahn D continuing to drive west. But, faced with farm roads, he diverted north again, this time toward Malmédy. At Baugnez Crossroads, as is now writ large in history, Peiper's spearhead encountered a U.S. convoy, and as he headed off to Ligneuville, little did he know what his following Kampfgruppe would do to those prisoners. When the rest of KG Peiper came up the road the infamous massacre took place.

Above and Below Left: *Vehicles parked in a farmyard close to the crossroads. 3rd FJR Div had made the initial breakthrough south of Losheim and one of its units—I./FJR 9—was subordinated to LSSAH. Some of its men, carried by King Tiger 222, will be seen in various photos through the book. Infiltration of Honsfeld saw units of Operation Greif involved. The After Action Report of 801st TD Bn mentions a number of incidents including: "At 04:00A the 2nd plat of Coy A with three 3" guns reported to its Coy HQ that one American light tank with German occupants had slipped by its gun position and a bazooka team consisting of the plat leader and two men were trying to intercept the tank and destroy it. As the bazooka team moved down the road they noted a convoy of German tanks and vehicles had joined up with the American light tank and all were heading in the direction of HONSFELD. It was also noted that the Germans on the light tank were speaking English."*

Battery B of the 285th Artillery Observation Battalion was in a convoy of some thirty vehicles and 140 men. The SS shot up the convoy, forcing the men to hide in ditches. Peiper was nearby and approved of the order to cease firing and just herd the prisoners off to the side. What actually happened at Malmédy has been debated since 1944. It seems unlikely that Peiper himself gave direct orders to initiate the massacre, but postwar attempts to obfuscate the issue cannot hide the enormity of what happened. After the massacre at Malmédy, eighty-four bodies were found. They had been cold-bloodedly murdered by the SS.

The American War Memorial lies at Baugnez crossroads, the tablet reads: "To the memory of the United States soldiers who while prisoners of war were massacred by Nazi troops on this spot on 17 December 1944." The black markers identify the dead.

1 *Aerial view of the American War Memorial at Baugnez crossroads. The field where the massacre took place is at A.*

2 *One of a sequence of graphic photographs of the scene.*

3 *Lt Col Hal McCown—captured by LSSAH and confined in cellars in La Gleize—gives his evidence at the postwar trial of Peiper and members of Leibstandarte.*

This Page: *There were other atrocities. Here, the memorial to the Wereth 11, artillerymen of the 333rd FA Bn, tortured and murdered by men of LSSAH's KG Knittel. The memorial was originally erected by Herman Langer, the son of the farmer, who had given the men food and shelter in the corner of the pasture where they were murdered. The family's role is also remembered (below).*

Jochen Peiper
(1915 –1976)

He preferred Jochen to Joachim, saying it sounded less Jewish. He was the consummate SS hero whose wartime exploits made him at once a hero among ordinary Germans and a murderer to others. At just nineteen he joined the SS-VT, went through two years of officer training, and in 1936 was posted to the Leibstandarte. Peiper spent the first wartime campaign in Poland, as part of Hitler's staff, saw action with Leibstandarte in 1940 in France, during which he led the assault on the Wattenberg Heights and was awarded the Iron Cross 1st class for his actions. For a long period he commanded the 3/SS-PzGr-Regt 2, and established an outstanding reputation as a combat leader. In 1943 he won the Knight's Cross at Kharkov. In 1944, he led the spearhead of the German Ardennes offensive. Subsequently promoted to SS-Standartenführer, commanding SS-Pz-Regt1, he was the youngest regimental colonel in the Waffen-SS. Implicated in massacres in France, Russia, and at Malmédy, postwar he was sentenced to hang, but the sentence was commuted and he was released from prison in 1956. Finding life in postwar Germany incompatible with his fervent Nazi beliefs, in 1970 he moved to France. He was murdered at his home on Bastille Day in July 1976.

Opposite, Above: *"We captured 200,000 liters in Büllingen and used fifty American prisoners to fill all of our tanks. This was a lucky break, because by the time we had reached Losheim, we had used up as much gasoline in 25 kilometers as we would normally have used in covering 50 kilometers, on account of the mountainous terrain in the Eifel,"* Peiper said postwar. *"... this was a clean breakthrough, and we continued with very little opposition."* Büllingen market square was where the fuel dump was. After the war it was planted and now sports a children's play area.

Opposite, Inset: *LSSAH Panther Ausf. G knocked out near the Baugnez Crossroads. It has suffered an explosive ammunition fire, evident from the blown-out sponson floor sitting on the tracks.*

Above Left: *Ligneuville. The Hotel du Moulin at left was vacated by Brig Gen Edward W. Timberlake of the 49th AAA Bde just in time. He left his breakfast on the table for Peiper to enjoy. LSSAH commander, Oberführer Wilhelm Mohnke, moved his forward CP here.*

Left: *German dead near Büllingen In the background of this graphic photos is one of the Jagdpanthers of sPzJgAbt 560 attached to Hitlerjugend. Should Peiper have continued north, attacking 2nd and 99th Division to help clear the Elsenborn Ridge defenses?*

Below: *The memorial at Ligneuville remembers the murder of eight prisoners of the 9th Armd Div shot near the Hotel du Moulin by the LSSAH advance guard.*

1

Dedicated To

**Company C
51st Engineer Combat Battalion
17-21 December, 1944**

The engineers at the Battle of Trois Ponts
stopped elements of the Sixth German
Panzer Army from breaking out to the
Meuse River, until reinforced by the
82nd Airborne Division.

Ⓐ

Ⓔ

Ⓑ

2

3

Amblève River

Peiper turns north
to La Gleize

Peiper advance

to Stavelot

Amblève bridge

Petit Spai bridge

**Anti-tank
gun**

E Co 505th PIR

Salm bridge

**Wanne
Heights**

Salm R.

Ⓓ

Lower
Salm bridge

TROIS PONTS

December, 1944

G Co 505th PIR

Ⓒ

1 and 3 *The Kampfgruppe reached Trois-Ponts on the road from Stavelot (**A**) looking for a bridge across the Amblève, but the 51st ECB blew both it (**B**) and the two bridges over the Salm (**C** and **D** on map). A plaque (**E**) commends C Coy, 51st ECB for their bravery. The first bridge (**F**) was close; the other (**G**) was some way south and Peiper had sent a small force past Wanne to come round on it from behind. They arrived too late. With his way barred, Peiper was forced to head north and, reaching La Gleize, tried to route via Cheneux and over the Lienne Creek. Held up by an air attack, the Kampfgruppe arrived at the bridge to see it blown up by 291st ECB. Peiper backtracked to La Gleize where he received the bad news that Stavelot had fallen to the Americans. The only way was forward towards Stoumont and a route to the Meuse via Huy. The attack would start on December 19.*

4 and 5 *The display board at Monceau on the heights above Cheneux is one of five linked boards in the area on the theme of the suffering of 1944, each with a wonderful illustration by Philippe Jarbinet. Note the Froidcour château in the distance at left.*

6 and 7 *One of the crucial moments on December 18 was the blowing of Neufmoulin bridge over the Lienne by "those damned engineers" —the 291st ECB. With this road blocked Peiper was forced to concentrate on the attack at Stoumont.*

KG Peiper crashed through Stavelot on the morning of December 18 thanks to the capture of the bridge intact. Once through Stavelot, the KG's next objective was Trois Points, which had three bridges, across both the Amblève and the Salm rivers, which met at that town. Unfortunately for Peiper, engineers blew the bridge in their faces as they did to two companies of PzKpfw IVs sent directly toward Trois-Ponts south of the Amblève. Peiper was forced to follow the Amblève northward and then west through the village of La Gleize over the bridge at Cheneux. The were held up just after the bridge by P-47 Thunderbolts which knocked out a Panther and at least half a dozen other vehicles. More important, the entire column lost two hours as it had to hunker down from the air assaults.

When Peiper finally reached the next water barrier in his path, Lienne Creek, once again U.S. engineers blew up the bridge in his path. Peiper was forced back to La Gleize where he resumed the advance through Stoumont. But by now some of the toughest divisions in the U.S. Army were converging on him. From the south, 82nd Airborne was assembling at Werbomont; from the north, CCB of the 3rd Armd Div had arrived, with attached artillery battalions; and the entire 30th Inf Div was now on the scene.

On a foggy December 19 Peiper took Stoumont, and 284 prisoners without trouble, but was held at Stoumont Station, a few kilometers beyond. Forced back, the fighting around Stoumont was intense but, inexorably, the Germans were pushed back to defensive positions around La Gleize. It was from there at about 02:00 on Christmas Eve, that Peiper's remaining able-bodied troops, numbering about 800, abandoned their vehicles and made their way to Wanne on foot.

Right: *Stymied at Habiémont with the blowing of the Neufmoulin Bridge, at 07:00 on December 19, Peiper's Kampfgruppe advanced towards Stoumont and, ultimately, Liège, some thirty miles to the northwest. The two WW2 images are stills from a film captured by the Americans and show the attack on Stoumont. Initially, the attack went well, albeit against stern defense by the 3rd Bn, 119th Inf Regt, 30th Inf Div who had been reinforced by ten M4s earlier that morning. By 11:00 the 119th had been forced back to Stoumont Station where the 1st Bn, 119th Inf Regt, reinforced by the 740th Tank Bn (the 119th's* Combat Journal *identifies a company of mediums and SP TDs) attacked and pushed Peiper back. The battle raged in Stoumont for the next two days, particularly around the key location, the Stoumont St. Edouard Sanatorium, until, on the afternoon of the 21st, Peiper pulled his force back and set up a defensive position around La Gleize.*

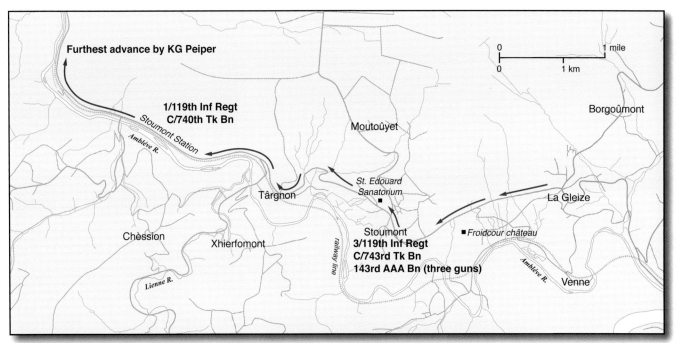

Furthest advance by KG Peiper

1/119th Inf Regt
C/740th Tk Bn

Stoumont Station

Amblève R.

Moutoûyet

St. Edouard
Sanatorium

Borgoûmont

Târghon

La Gleize

Chèssion

Xhierfomont

railway line

Stoumont
3/119th Inf Regt
C/743rd Tk Bn
143rd AAA Bn (three guns)

Froidcour château

Lienne R.

Amblève R.

Venne

TO ROAD NET
IN FOREST

SANATORIUM

STOUMONT

TO
LA GLEIZE

Above: *The progress of KG Peiper was stopped just past Stoumont by task forces of 3rd Armd Div.*

Left and Below: *The St. Edouard Sanatorium at Stoumont was the scene of heavy fighting.*

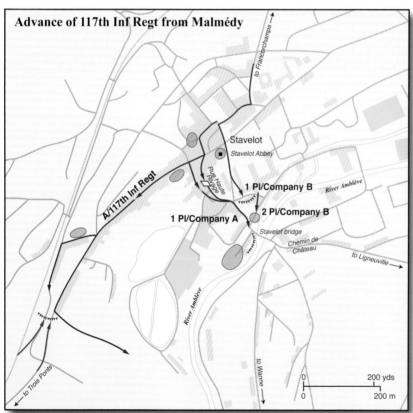

Advance of 117th Inf Regt from Malmédy

to Francorchamps

Stavelot

Stavelot Abbey

Rue Haute Rivage

1 Pl/Company B

River Amblève

2 Pl/Company B

1 Pl/Company A

Stavelot bridge

Chemin de Château

to Ligneuville

A/117th Inf Regt

River Amblève

to Trois Ponts

to Wanne

0   200 yds

0   200 m

Above and Above Right: *These aerial views face south. At* **A** *the bridge, which was intact when captured by Peiper—Operation Greif commandos having disabled the charges on it. The bridge was later blown during the battle. At* **B** *the location of the Tiger KO'd on the rue Haut-Rivage (***right***); at* **C** *the main square and battlefield marker; at* **D** *memorial wall next to Stavelot Abbey; at* **E** *Chemin du Château down which* Leibstandarte *advanced from Malmédy; at* **F** *the road to Trois-Ponts that KG Peiper took; at* **G** *the road to Wanne;* **H** *KO'd Tiger II No 222 (as seen on p. 96).*

Left: *Roosevelt's SS move into Stavelot. 117th Inf Regt of 30th Inf Div moved in after KG Peiper had motored through. They held it in the face of strong attacks and Peiper was unable to receive reinforcements or supplies through this key town.*

Center Right: *The fighting in Stavelot was intense.*

Right: *In Stavelot's rue Haut-Rivage (***B***) KG Peiper lost King Tiger turret number 105, the mount of company commander SS-Obersturmführer Jürgen Wessel of sPzAbt 501. It was hit on the mantlet, reversed into a building and was immobilized.*

Stavelot

Above: *Memorial to the men of 504th PIR who took Cheneux from KG Peiper and advanced towards La Gleize.*

Above Right: *Bazooka men of 82nd Airborne's C Coy, 325th GIR, await Kampfgruppe Peiper on December 20 at Werbomont.*

Right and Below Right: *504th PIR marches through Rahier towards Cheneux—note the white house through the trees at left in the today image.*

Opposite, Above: *Coy D, 2/504th PIR talk to the chaplain en route to relieve 1st Bn at Cheneux.*

Opposite, Below: *Airborne troop movements and advance December 20–25.*

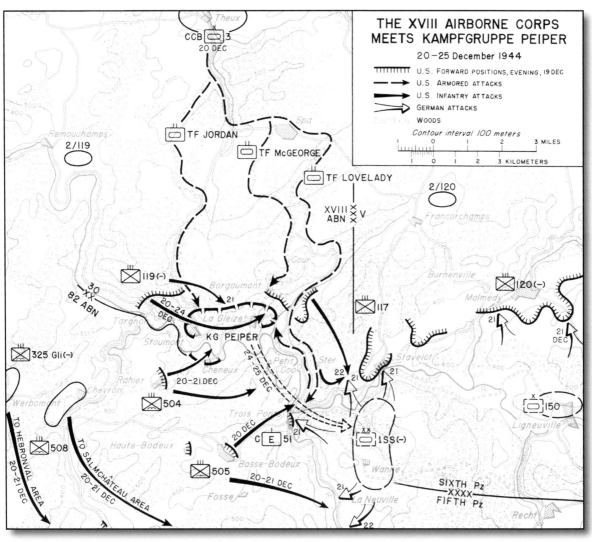

THE XVIII AIRBORNE CORPS
MEETS KAMPFGRUPPE PEIPER

20—25 December 1944

U.S. FORWARD POSITIONS, EVENING, 19 DEC
U.S. ARMORED ATTACKS
U.S. INFANTRY ATTACKS
GERMAN ATTACKS
WOODS

Contour interval 100 meters

KG Peiper fought until all fuel and food had gone, the only attempt to airdrop supplies fell mainly into American hands. Early in the morning of the 24th Peiper and some thousand men left a rearguard and the wounded and made a break for German lines, which they achieved successfully on the 25th. The vehicles left behind are analyzed carefully in Duel in the Mist 3 and included King Tigers 104 and 204, and in the near vicinity were four more King Tigers—213, 218, 221, and 334. In total Peiper left behind over fifty tanks and SP guns and seventy halftracks.

Today, the museum at La Gleize boasts a number of recovered exhibits including one of these King Tigers (turret number 213), which ended up outside the museum (**1**)—it was originally the presbytery and was used as an aid station. The town hall (**2** and **above**) had been used as a command post. The U.S. Army had intended to take King Tiger 213 home in July 1945, but the story goes that it was saved by the intervention of a local woman and a bottle of cognac! 213 was instead towed to the village square, and in August 1951, the Belgian Army moved it to its present position near the churchyard. The damage on the glacis was caused after capture when infantrymen tried to penetrate it.

Kaiserbaracke

These classic German photos of the Ardennes come from film captured in late December by the Americans. A mixture of action photos and staged shots, they include a number taken at Kaiserbaracke crossroads in the Wolfbusch Forest. Frequently captioned as being of Jochen Peiper, painstaking investigative work by After the Battle proved the images to be of another unit, probably the reconnaissance battalion of Leibstandarte on the morning of December 18. The King Tiger, number 222, is seen at various locations on the march. The troops hitching a ride are Fallschirmjäger from I./FJR 9. Today, the area is covered by a business park and there is no meaningful photographic comparison. The King Tigers of SS-sPzAbt 501 proved pretty ineffective in the terrain around Stavelot, Trois-Ponts, and La Gleize. They broke down the whole time, had problems on the narrow muddy roads, and couldn't use most of the bridges because of their weight. Of the forty-five at the start, only six kept up with KG Peiper.

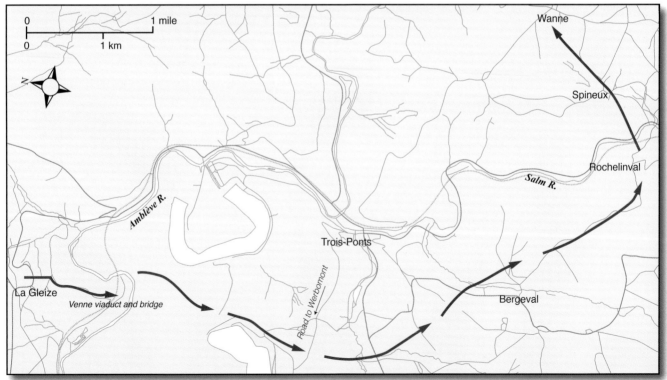

Opposite, Above: *In the end, lacking fuel and ammunition, and under continuous artillery bombardment, Peiper left La Gleize and his heavy weapons, 135 armored vehicles in total including six Tiger IIs: 334 on the Borgoûmont road (seen here); 104 and 204 in the village; and 221 and 213 on the high ground near Wérimont Farm. The latter, SS-Obersturmführer Wilhelm Dollinger's Tiger II number 213, can be seen today by La Gleize church. Finally, 332 was found at Coo and transported to the United States. Additionally, nearly fifty SPWs, seven PzKpfw IVs, thirteen PzKpfw Vs, six Bisons (150mm hows), three Pumas, a Flakpanzer IV, and a Flak halftrack were left behind.*

Left: *The rail viaduct at Venne and the footbridge over the Amblève crossed by the remnants of KG Peiper as they retreated. The map (**Opposite, Below**) shows the escape path.*

Below Left: *KG Hansen set up its HQ in the chateau at Wanne, where it was joined by Sepp Dietrich. The village was subsequently liberated by the 517th Parachute RCT as shown in the memorial (**Below**).*

7 St. Vith

A classic photo of M4s of the 40th Tank Bn, 7th Armd Div, in temporary positions near St. Vith, firing on enemy positions beyond the city.

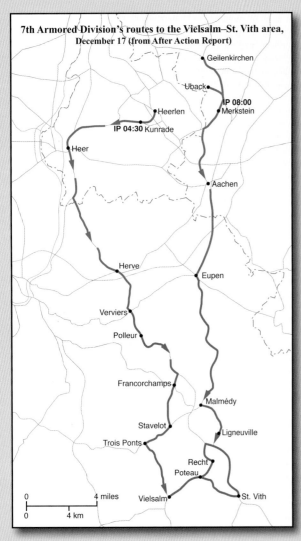

7th Armored Division's routes to the Vielsalm–St. Vith area, December 17 (from After Action Report)

Geilenkirchen

Uback

Heerlen

IP 08:00 Merkstein

IP 04:30 Kunrade

Heer

Aachen

Herve

Eupen

Verviers

Polleur

Francorchamps

Malmédy

Stavelot

Ligneuville

Trois Ponts

Recht

Poteau

Vielsalm

St. Vith

0   4 miles
0   4 km

Above: *The route of 7th Armd Div to the St. Vith area: West Route (left) 87th Cavalry Recon Sqn, CCB, CCA, 814th TD Bn, Div HQ, 33rd Armd Engr Bn, Div Trains. East Route (right) CCR, Div Tac, Div Artillery, 203rd AAA AW Bn, B/129th Armd Ord Maint Bn.*

The attack on the Schnee Eifel led to the surrender of large parts of 106th Inf Div and the exodus of whatever forces were able to get away. Over 7,000 GIs entered captivity—Cole suggests the figure could have been as high as 9,000. It was one of the worst defeats U.S. forces have ever endured and, to make it worse, it wasn't caused by crack enemy troops and heavy armor—the attackers were also "green," including Luftwaffe field troops.

It's not very difficult to isolate what happened: inexperienced and poorly trained troops simply weren't well led. Also, as if this wasn't bad enough, strategic errors higher up the command chain left the Losheim Gap poorly defended, and the inclement weather prohibited air support. On top of this, the units sent to help—particularly 7th Armd Div—had a sixty-plus-mile trip down from Geilenkirchen and the timetable for this move went awry—not that any blame could attach to the "Lucky Seventh": their advance party left the division CP within two hours of being notified to move. However, reaching Vielsalm by 11:00 on the 17th, Brig Gen Bruce Clark's CCB was hampered severely by the mass of vehicles moving west—it would take Gen. Hasbrouck (7th Armd Div's CG) five hours to make the same journey. When he got there he discovered that 106th's CG—Maj-Gen Alan W. Jones—had handed over command to Clark (Jones was not a well man. He would have a heart attack in January).

Had the Germans made a concerted effort to attack St. Vith immediately there's no doubt it would have fallen. By the time they did, a defense had been cobbled together by 7th Armd Div, CCB of 9th Armd Div, the 424th Infantry and other remnants of 106th Inf Div, and the 112th Infantry of the 28th Inf Div.

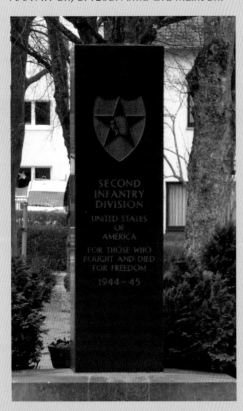

Opposite, Below L–R: *St. Vith memorials—to the 2nd Inf Div* (**left**)*, 106th Division* (**center**)*, and the 168th ECB* (**right**)*. The 106th was encircled on the Schnee Eifel losing two of its regiments to captivity; the remnants joined the defenders of St. Vith. The 2nd Inf Div fought on the Elsenborn Ridge 168th ECB fought as part of CCB 7th Armd Div.*

This Page: *Vehicles of 48th Inf Bn, 7th Armd Div in St. Vith. The division was fundamental to the defense of St. Vith and helped delay the German advance before withdrawing west of the Salm River on December 23. The 7th then took part in the battles around Manhay. "By their epic stand, without prepared defenses and despite heavy casualties ... inflicted crippling losses and imposed great delay upon the enemy by a masterful and grimly determined defense."*

CCB 7th Armd Div won a Presidential Unit Citation. After defending Manhay and Grandmenil the division was taken out of the line to refit before spearheading the retaking of St. Vith, January 20–28, 1945.

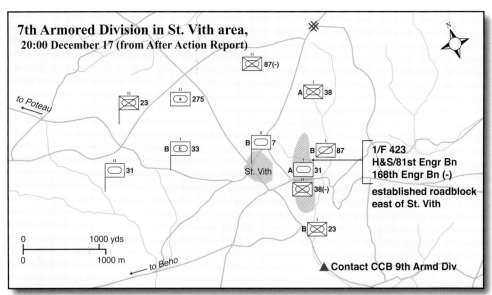

7th Armored Division in St. Vith area,
20:00 December 17 (from After Action Report)

to Poteau

87(-)

A 38

23

275

B E 33

B 7

B 87

St. Vith

A 31

31

38(-)

1/F 423
H&S/81st Engr Bn
168th Engr Bn (-)

established roadblock
east of St. Vith

0   1000 yds
0   1000 m

to Beho

B 23

▲ Contact CCB 9th Armd Div

The defense held up Fifth Panzerarmee from December 17 until St. Vith finally fell on the 21st, the defenders escaping west through a corridor held open by 82nd Airborne. The Germans may have won a significant tactical victory, but the defenders of St. Vith, particularly the 7th Armd Div and remnants of the 106th, had derailed their schedule,

Above and Opposite, Inset: *Like St-Lô and Caen before it, St. Vith suffered from both Allied and German bombardments during the Ardennes Offensive. After it was captured by the Germans, the town was bombed heavily over Xmas by the USAAF and by RAF Bomber Command, the latter staging a very heavy attack on December 26, with 274 bombers striking at the immediate vicinity.*

Above Right: *The defense of St. Vith on the 17th. Both sides suffered from traffic problems— the Allies were trying to get 7th Armd Div in place; the Germans were rushing the Führer Begleit Brigade into the attack from reserve, but the U.S. defenders got in place first. They held out until the 21st by which time the bulk of U.S. forces had retreated. The final attack was bolstered by Tiger IIs of sPzAbt 506. This unit started with forty-one Tigers and attacked from the northern edge of the Schnee Eifel, through the 14th Cavalry Group. It advanced towards Schönberg where it ensured that the encircled U.S. forces couldn't break out before continuing on to St. Vith where it helped destroy the 7th Armd Div roadblock while supporting 18th VG Division. The unit then moved south to Bastogne.* (See also p. 171.)

Right: *A composite photo showing a German column advancing along the road from Winterspelt to St. Vith. The lack of leaves on the trees meant that camouflage was difficult and white paint was in short supply.*

so much so that von Manteuffel told Hitler that they should immediately return to the Westwall. Hitler disagreed and the German advance continued but it had to fight for every inch of ground, and every crossroads saw a pitched battle until Fifth Panzerarmee was halted close to the Meuse, where British troops were involved at the close. The central attack may have got farther than elsewhere, but the defense of St. Vith ensured that Fifth Panzerarmee wouldn't reach the Meuse.

Right: *Maj Gen "Pete" Quesada, IX TAC of U.S. Ninth Air Force, visits St. Vith after it was retaken in January 1945 and surveys the damage. When Eisenhower placed the northern U.S. forces under British command, Quesada's IX TAC was put under "Maori" Coningham's British 2TAF. Coningham placed his British aircraft at Quesada's disposal as Quesada was, "closest to the scene of activity, ... in the best position to draw up the plan and exercise close control of the important air phase of the Bulge Battle."*

Opposite, Above left: C Coy, 23rd AIB, Hunnage, near St. Vith. As part of CCB, 23rd AIB was one of the units that received the Presidential Unit Citation for "outstanding performance of duty in action from 17 to 23 December 1944, inclusive, at St. Vith, Belgium ... By their epic stand, without prepared defenses and despite heavy casualties, Combat Command B, 7th Armd Div, inflicted crippling losses and imposed great delay upon the enemy by a masterful and grimly determined defense."

Opposite, Above right: A dug-in mortar emplacement, 48th AIB, 7th Armd Div, St. Vith. Each battalion had an 81mm Mortar Platoon of an HQ section and three mortar squads.

Opposite, Center Left: Soldiers of the 23rd AIB crawl forward trying to avoid a sniper's fire.

Opposite, Center Right: Easy Coy, 2nd Bn, 117th Regt, 30th Division, St. Vith.

Above Left: Men of 460th Parachute FA Battalion, serving with 517th RCT, an element of the 17th Airborne Division. The RCT was split up and saw action with 3rd and 7th Armd, 30th and 106th Inf, and 82nd Airborne divisions. It gave a good account of itself and could boast a Presidential Distinguished Unit Citation for its action around Soy–Hotton, Belgium during which Pfc Melvin E. Biddle of B Coy, 1/517th PIR was awarded the Medal of Honor (see p. 145).

Left: The fall of St. Vith saw one of the few times that Tigers (in this case Tiger IIs) were used to effect in the Ardennes, but they couldn't prevent some 15,000 men and about a hundred tanks escaping to bolster 82nd Airborne in the defense. The Germans chased them, attacking in a front from Vielsalm and the Salm River to the crossroads at Baraque. By the night of December 23, 2nd SS-Panzer had taken the Baraque de Fraiture crossroads, and their next objective was the Manhay crossroads five miles away.

Poteau

This spread: *After having turned south at Kaiserbaracke Leibstandarte's KG Hansen caught CCR of 7th Armd Div near the Poteau crossroads and this famous set of photos shows the aftermath of the engagement on December 18. Today, a roadside marker remembers the incident (*Left*). Note the markings on the M8 (*Opposite, Below*): 1 A 18 C—First Army, 18th Cavalry Recon Sqn. Max Hansen's Kampfgruppe was nearly as strong as Peiper's, with 4,500 men and 750 vehicles. Except that instead of tanks he had a battalion of twenty-one Jagdpanzer IV/70s (*Opposite, Top*)—a good enough cudgel. Hansen had made excellent progress from the start, and after shooting up elements of the U.S. 14th Cavalry Group and 7th Armd Div's CCR around Poteau, he broke into the clear on Rollbahn E, just south of Peiper. It appeared he could drive all the way to Vielsalm on the Salm River, with untold consequences for the U.S. concentration at St. Vith; however, on December 18 orders arrived for him to pause at the village of Recht to wait for the 9th SS-Panzer Division Hohenstaufen to close up. KG Hansen thus spent the entire day of the 19th waiting for a second-wave division to squeeze through the gigantic traffic jams that characterized the army's entire rear area.*

This spread: *More Poteau photos, including the well-known sequence showing an SS-Schütze MG42-gunner holding a 9mm Browning High-Power, with two Fallschirmjäger and captured American cigarettes. The modern photo shows the Poteau crossroads and the museum. The photos are carefully examined in* Battle of the Bulge Then and Now *which identifies the American losses as being three M5s, six M8 Greyhounds, three halftracks, and eight jeeps. Task Force Myers made it back to the crossroads and set up a defensive position. They were overrun but KG Hansen did not take its opportunity to advance on Vielsalm. CCA/7th Armd Div retook the crossroads on the 18th and was then attacked by Kampfgruppe Telkamp from 9th SS-Panzer Division.*

Left: *The crossroads today.*

Below: *Aerial view of the ambush area. The vehicles have been pushed off the road. As Pallud points out, there are also three burnt-out Panthers which were destroyed in the fighting between CCA/7th Armd Div and KG Telkamp. The fighting continued until the 24th when CCA became the last major northerly unit to retreat through Vielsalm.*

Vielsalm

Above: *7th Armd Div defenses alongside the railroad bridge at Vielsalm. General Hasbrouck set up his CP in the town.*

Below Right: *Vielsalm's Square General Bruce C. Clarke and 7th Armd Div memorial.*

Below: *Memorial at Goronne: To our brave friends the brave men of the 508th Parachute Infantry Regiment of the 82nd Airborne Div. May our friendship be everlasting between the United States and Belgium. From the people of the Ardennes.*

Opposite, Above: *Realignment of U.S. positions December 20–23.*

On December 20 Field Marshal Montgomery took control of the Allied armies in the north of the battlefield. He immediately sent out his "Phantom" officers, specially trained liaison officers, to assess the situation. Ridgway, XVIII Airborne Corps commander, wanted to stand and fight. This was partly sheer stubbornness, but also partly training: airborne units expect to be surrounded and fighting in encircled positions and do not fear them. Hasbrouck, CG of 7th Armd Div, agreed with Monty; so did First Army commander Courtney Hodges.

The order came through on December 22 in the nick of time. With the Germans at their heels but hindered by traffic jams, and helped by a cold snap which hardened up the escape trail, 7th Armd Div, CCB of 9th Armd Div, and 424th Infantry extricated themselves while CCA/7th and CCR/7th maintained a rearguard. At 13:45 CCA dashed down the road to the Vielsalm bridge; CCR's turn came after CCA crossed (at around 16:20).

As well as ordering the withdrawal of 7th Armd Div, Monty moved XXX Corps to protect the Meuse bridges and assembled a counterattack force under Maj Gen J. Lawton Collins' VII Corps. It would consist of 84th Inf Div which Bradley had ordered down from Ninth Army, 75th Inf Div newly arrived from the U.S., and 3rd Armd Div. Collins would also get 2nd Armd Div from Ninth Army reserve.

Finally, and most contentiously, Monty pulled the line back to a more organized position, preferring to give up ground to ensure a manageable front. As the map (opposite) shows, this provided a defensive line that held.

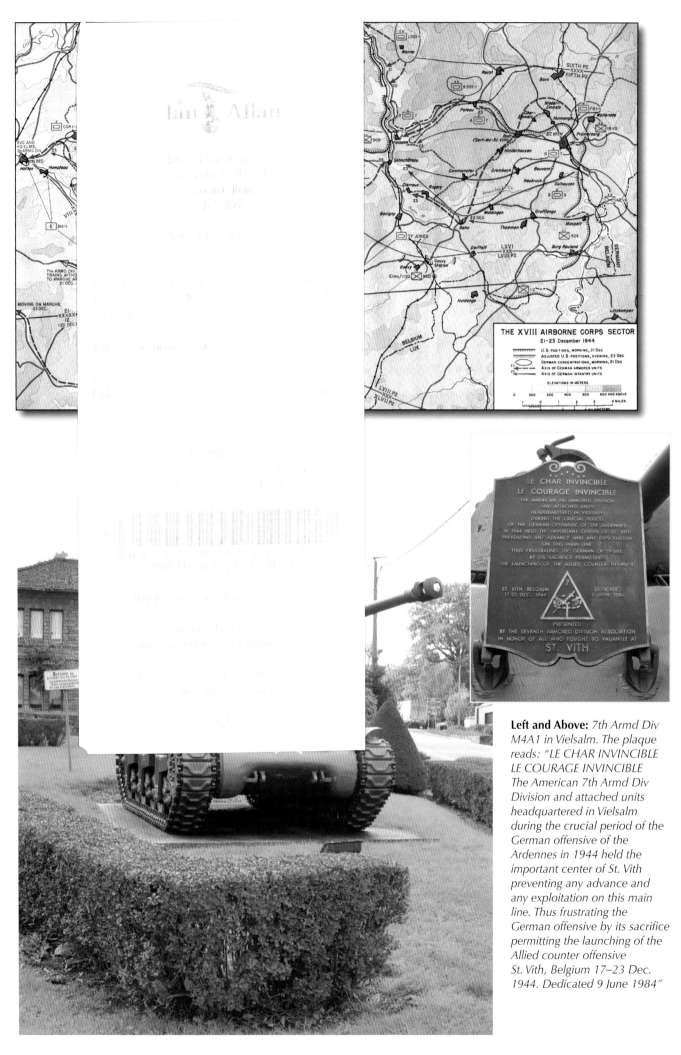

THE XVIII AIRBORNE CORPS SECTOR
21–23 December 1944

LE CHAR INVINCIBLE
LE COURAGE INVINCIBLE
THE AMERICAN 7th ARMORED DIVISION
AND ATTACHED UNITS
HEADQUARTERED IN VIELSALM
DURING THE CRUCIAL PERIOD
OF THE GERMAN OFFENSIVE OF THE ARDENNES
IN 1944 HELD THE IMPORTANT CENTER OF ST VITH
PREVENTING ANY ADVANCE AND ANY EXPLOITATION
ON THIS MAIN LINE
THUS FRUSTRATING THE GERMAN OFFENSIVE
BY ITS SACRIFICE PERMITTING
THE LAUNCHING OF THE ALLIED COUNTER-OFFENSIVE

ST. VITH, BELGIUM   DEDICATED
17-23 DEC. 1944   9 JUNE 1984

PRESENTED
BY THE SEVENTH ARMORED DIVISION ASSOCIATION
IN HONOR OF ALL WHO FOUGHT SO VALIANTLY AT
ST. VITH

Left and Above: *7th Armd Div M4A1 in Vielsalm. The plaque reads: "LE CHAR INVINCIBLE LE COURAGE INVINCIBLE The American 7th Armd Div Division and attached units headquartered in Vielsalm during the crucial period of the German offensive of the Ardennes in 1944 held the important center of St. Vith preventing any advance and any exploitation on this main line. Thus frustrating the German offensive by its sacrifice permitting the launching of the Allied counter offensive St. Vith, Belgium 17–23 Dec. 1944. Dedicated 9 June 1984"*

8 BASTOGNE

This Page: *Winter living out in the open sorted out the men from the boys! Hot food was essential, but the M1 carbine is at the ready.*

A number of U.S. units were ordered to Bastogne. From the north, the 705th Tank Bn had to dodge panzer spearheads en route. Various independent engineer and field artillery battalions were also ordered to the town, including the African-American 969th FA. From the south, Patton was ordered to send his 10th Armd Div. He didn't want to, but did release the division's CCB, which at Bastogne was broken into three task forces (Team Desobry went to Noville; Team Cherry to Longvilly, and Team O'Hara to Marvie), to intercept any enemy that arrived. Late on the 18th XLVII Panzerkorps (2nd Panzer Div) reached Noville, and ran into Task Force Desobry. Together with remnants of 9th Armd Div and survivors of the 28th Inf Div, the Tiger Division tankers were able to beat back the initial assault. A key to the German offensive was that it was launched in dismal weather, which kept Allied air forces out of the battle. But that same factor wreaked havoc on the roads, causing gigantic traffic jams that slowed German infantry and artillery support. One more day and Bastogne would be easy picking for the Germans. However, during the dark, early morning hours of December 19 the 101st Airborne arrived at the town.

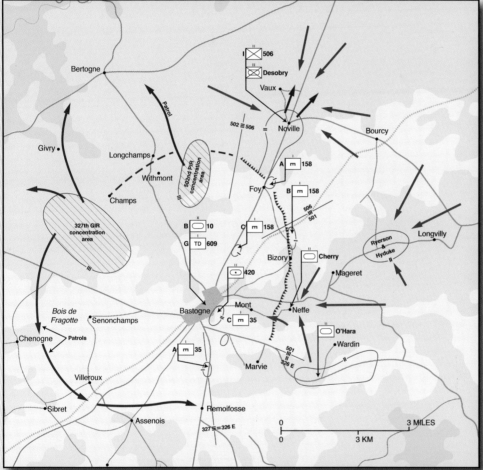

Above: *Elements of 110th Regt, 28th Inf Div who reached Bastogne at the beginning of the siege, regroup on December 20. They become part of "Team Snafu" along with stragglers from VIII Corps and elements of 9th Armd Div, under the command of 10th Armd Div's Col Roberts.*

Left: *The situation on December 19 shows the defense perimeter and enemy attacks on Noville, Longvilly, and Neffe—usually small German combined-arms forces, sometimes with artillery support, infiltrating under cover of bad weather with the support of tanks. On the most southerly of XLVII Panzerkorps' two Roll-bahns, 2nd Panzer Div skirted Bastogne and headed west leaving the town to be taken by 26th VG Division.*

Below: *The German forces prepare to attack 3rd/501st PIR on the night of December 20. They were repulsed by the paratroopers and a platoon of B/705th TD Bn which destroyed three SP guns,*

Right: *The 57mm Gun M1 was the primary U.S. antitank gun, with over 57,000 being produced between 1942–45, and two-thirds of which went to U.S. Army divisions in Europe. It was based on the British 6-pdr Mark II.*

Above: *The 155mm howitzers of the 969th FA Bn dug in, December 17. Artillery played an important role in the siege, particularly against armor. On December 20, for example, seven battalions fired 2,600 rounds solely at German armor.*

Right: *The order of battle shows that in the end there were around 22,800 men defending Bastogne. Stragglers found their way to Bastogne, even though the noose around the town tightened. They included artillery that would prove invaluable during the siege— 9th Armd Div's 73rd, the 58th, and the 969th Fd Arty Bns, the latter a 155mm unit—and a platoon from 705th TD Bn.*

ORDER OF BATTLE OF THE FORCES IN BASTOGNE

Under the command of acting 101st Division commander: Brig Gen Anthony C. McAuliffe
Asst CO: Brig Gen Gerald J. Higgins

101st Airborne Division
501st Parachute Infantry Regiment
  (Lt Col Julian J. Ewell)
502nd Parachute Infantry Regiment
  (Lt Col Steve A. Chappuis)
506th Parachute Infantry Regiment
  (Col Robert F. Sink)
327th Glider Infantry Regiment
  (Col Joseph H. Harper)
321st Glider Field Artillery Battalion
  (Lt Col Edward L. Carmichael)
907th Glider Field Artillery Battalion
  (Lt Col Clarence F. Nelson)
377th Parachute Field Artillery Battalion
  (Lt Col Harry W. Elkins)
463rd Parachute Field Artillery Battalion
  (Lt Col John T. Cooper, Jr.)
81st Airborne Antiaircraft Battalion
  (Lt Col X. B. Cox, Jr.)
326th Airborne Engineer Battalion
  (Lt Col Hugh A. Mozley)

**Combat Command B, 10th Armored
  Division** (Col William L. Roberts)
3rd Tank Battalion (Lt Col Henry T. Cherry)
20th Armored Infantry Battalion
  (Maj William R. Desobry)
54th Armored Infantry Battalion
  (Lt Col James O'Hara)
420th Armored Field Artillery Battalion
  (Lt Col Barry D. Browne)

705th Tank Destroyer Battalion
  (Lt Col Clifford D. Templeton)
755th Field Artillery Battalion
969th Field Artillery Battalion

Other troops
35th and 158th Combat Engineer Battalions;
  58th and 420th Armored Field Artillery
  Battalions
Team SNAFU (mainly stragglers from 28th Inf
  Div)

Right and Below Right: *A January 16 view of Foy just after the 101st Airborne arrived.*

Below: *Team Desobry of 10th Armd Div had been sent to Noville, just north of Foy on the Houffalize road, getting there at around 23:00 on December 18. When 101st Airborne arrived in Bastogne, 1st Bn 506th PIR under Lt Col LaPrade was sent to assist, arriving around midday on the 19th. 2nd and 3rd Bns 506th PIR were in reserve just north of Bastogne on the Noville road. Desobry and LaPrade set up a CP in this house and fought a delaying action allowing the defense perimeter to be set up around Bastogne. Eventually, an 88mm round exploded in the house, killing LaPrade and wounding Desobry who was taken to hospital. He was taken prisoner by the Germans when the field hospital was captured (see caption opposite). Maj Robert F. Harwick took command of the combined force with the armor coming under the command of Maj Charles L. Hustead. Serjos de Groot/TracesOfWar.com*

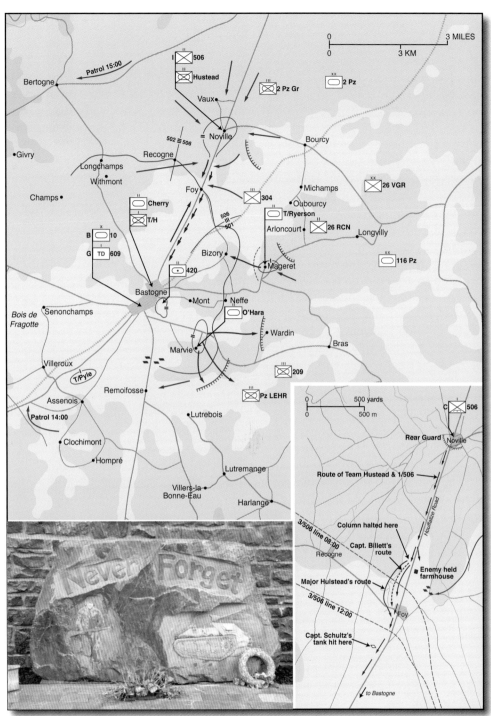

Left: *December 20: the attacks intensify. Overnight, the 101st had lost its field hospital, over-run by an attack. The aid station of the 501st PIR in Bastogne took over medical duties until a glider on December 26 brought in a surgical team. Team Desobry—now Team Hustead under command of Maj Charles L. Hustead—and the 1st/506th under Maj Bob Hardwick, withdrew from Noville. The column was ambushed at Foy, the road blocked, and a number of men killed before they fought their way back to Luzery. There was no rest to be had as the unit was almost immediately sent to Bois Jacques.*

Below: *Views of Noville then and now. The memorial below remembers Lt Gen William Desobry—then a major—whose 10th Armd Div task force defended Noville. Desobry was wounded, taken prisoner, and ended up imprisoned in Fallingbostel. Liberated in the spring of 1945, he served until 1975 in diverse roles, including CG of the Armor Center and Armor School at Fort Knox, KY, and commander of V Corps based in Frankfurt.*

Left: *"Never Forget," memorial to those who fought in Noville.*

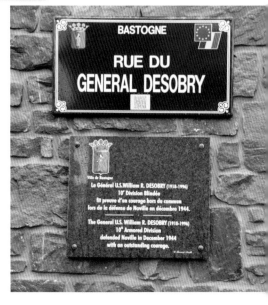

Nuts!

Above: *As Maxwell Taylor was at a staff meeting in the U.S. when the Germans attacked, so assistant divisional commander, Brig Gen Anthony C. McAuliffe took command. For his actions at Bastogne, he was awarded the Distinguished Service Cross on December 30, 1944, followed later by the Distinguished Service Medal. On January 15, 1945, he was promoted to major-general and given command of the 103rd Inf Div. He continued in service after the war, retiring in 1956.*

At 11:30 on December 22, four Germans approached American lines south of Bastogne. The senior officer explained that they had a written message to be presented to the American commander of the town. They were taken first to the Kessler farmhouse and then to the F/327th GIR Command Post from where the message went to the Battalion Command Post in Marvie, then the 327th HQ and finally to Division HQ. Acting Chief of Staff, Lt Col Ned Moore entered Brig Gen Anthony C. McAuliffe's sleeping quarters and told him, "The Germans have sent some people forward to take our surrender." Moore recalled that McAuliffe, still half asleep, said "Nuts!" and started to climb out of his sleeping bag. The Division Operations Officer, Lt Col Harry Kinnard, remembered later that McAuliffe initially asked, "They want to surrender?" Moore told him, "No sir, they want us to surrender." McAuliffe erupted in anger, which shocked those looking on. He took the paper, looked at it, said, "Us surrender, aw nuts!" and dropped it on the floor. A little later he was informed that the German officers were still waiting for a formal reply at the F Company Command Post. McAuliffe wondered aloud, "Well, I don't know what to tell them." Kinnard said, "What you said initially would be hard to beat ... Sir, you said nuts." All members of the staff enthusiastically agreed, so McAuliffe said, "Have it typed up."

The 327th PIR commander, Col Joseph W. Harper, took the reply and informed the senior German officer that he had the American Commander's reply. The German—who was blindfolded—asked if the reply was affirmative. Harper said, "The reply consists of a single word: Nuts! ... If you continue this foolish attack, your losses will be tremendous."

The two blindfolded German officers were then driven back to the Kessler farm. At the farm, the blindfolds were removed and the Germans opened the reply but didn't understand it. "What does this mean?"

"You can go to Hell," said Harper, who went on, "If you continue to attack, we will kill every goddamn German that tries to break into this city." The German replied, "We will kill many Americans. This is war." Harper then said, "On your way Bud, and good luck to you."

McAuliffe turned the incident to good advantage, providing his command with a Christmas message shown below.

---

24 December 1944

Merry Christmas!
HEADQUARTERS, 101st AIRBORNE DIVISION
Office of the Division Commander

What's merry about all this, you ask? We're fighting – it's cold – we aren't home. All true, but what has the proud Eagle Division accomplished with its worthy comrades of the 10th Armored Division, the 705th Tank Destroyer Battalion and all the rest? Just this: We have stopped cold everything that has been thrown at us from the North, East, South, and West. We have identifications from four German Panzer Divisions, two German Infantry Divisions and one German Parachute Division. These units, spearheading the last desperate German lunge, were headed straight west for key points when the Eagle Division was hurriedly ordered to stem the advance. How effectively this was done will be written in history; not alone in our Division's glorious history but in world history. The Germans actually did surround us, their radios blared our doom. Their Commander demanded our surrender in the following impudent arrogance:

December 22d 1944

"To the U.S.A. Commander of the encircled town of Bastogne:
"The fortune of war is changing. This time the U.S.A. forces in and near Bastogne have been encircled by strong German armored units. More German armored units have crossed the river Ourthe near Ortheuville, have taken Marche and reached St. Hubert by passing through Hompre–Sibret–Tillet. Libramont is in German hands.

"There is only one possibility to save the encircled U.S.A. troops from total annihilation: that is the honorable surrender of the encircled town. In order to think it over a term of two hours will be granted beginning with the presentation of this note.

"If this proposal should be rejected one German Artillery Corps and six heavy A. A. Battalions are ready to annihilate the U.S.A. troops in and near Bastogne. The order for firing will be given immediately after this two hours' term.

"All the serious civilian losses caused by this artillery fire would not correspond with the well-known American humanity.

The German Commander"

The German Commander received the following reply:

22 December 1944

"To The German Commander:
N U T S!
The American Commander"

Allied Troops are counterattacking in force. We continue to hold Bastogne. By holding Bastogne we assure the success of the Allied Armies. We know that our Division Commander, General Taylor, will say: "Well Done!"

We are giving our country and our loved ones at home a worthy Christmas present and being privileged to take part in this gallant feat of arms are truly making for ourselves a Merry Christmas.

A. C. McAuliffe
Commanding

Left and Center left: *Another view of 1st Bn, 506th PIR heading out to Noville to support Team Desobry. With pressure from command to push beyond Bastogne, German Fifth Panzer Army and XLVII Corps decided that Panzer Lehr should take Bastogne while the other forces continued west. The envelopment of Bastogne was completed on the 21st, but as Mitchell says, "Though surrounded, the 101st was not cut off." Panzer Lehr didn't accomplish its mission on December 20th and tried again with 26th VG Division on the 21st. The perimeter tightened, but held, and on the night of the 21st Manteuffel and XVLII Korps commander, Heinrich Freiherr von Lüttwitz, decided to send a letter to the commander of the Bastogne garrison.*

Below: *Taken towards the end of the battle in January 1945 this looks down the road towards Longvilly. These vehicles belonged to Team Cherry, commanded by Lt Col Henry T. Cherry, 3rd Tank Bn, 10th Armd Div). Reinforced by 501st PIR on December 18, for the next two days Team Cherry held up Panzer Lehr Division and Bayerlein's XLVII Panzer Corps.*

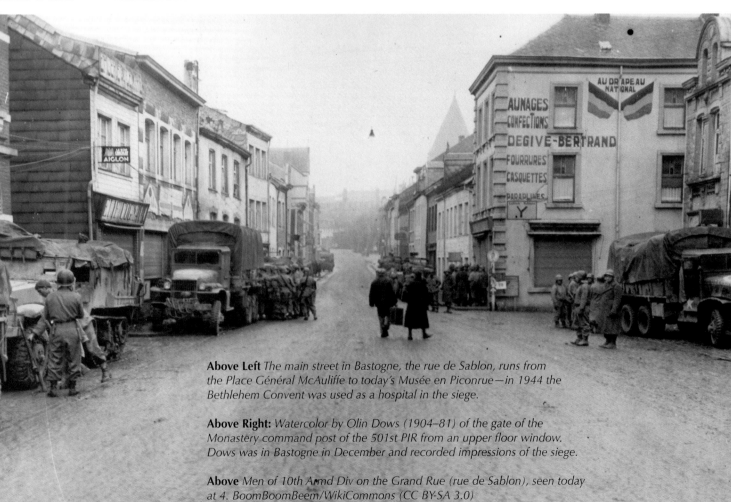

Above Left *The main street in Bastogne, the rue de Sablon, runs from the Place Général McAuliffe to today's Musée en Piconrue—in 1944 the Bethlehem Convent was used as a hospital in the siege.*

Above Right: *Watercolor by Olin Dows (1904–81) of the gate of the Monastery command post of the 501st PIR from an upper floor window. Dows was in Bastogne in December and recorded impressions of the siege.*

Above *Men of 10th Armd Div on the Grand Rue (rue de Sablon), seen today at 4. BoomBoomBeem/WikiCommons (CC BY-SA 3.0)*

Above and Below: *Then and now aerial views of Bastogne.*
1 identifies the road running north and is visible at the lower
left of the aerial recon photo. 2 identifies the main square, and
3 the course of the rue de Sablon.

Above: *Refugees evacuating Bastogne. They are in the main square now named after Brig Gen Anthony McAuliffe.*

Right and Opposite, Top *Then and now photos of Place Général McAuliffe. The round building on the today image is the tourist center. Note the M4A3 Sherman by the intersection. Named Barracuda, it served in Coy B, 41st Tank Bn, 11th Armd Div. It was knocked out near Renaumont, west of Bastogne, on December 30.*

Opposite, Below: *Memorials in the square are to 11th Armd Div (2) and Gen McAuliffe (3).*

GENERAL
McAULIFFE

A and C *Bois Jacques—Jack's Wood—Band of Brothers. The plaque on the monument (right) reads:*

"May the world never forget. In the wood behind this monument, on 18 December 1944 'E' Company of the 506th PIR 101st Airborne Division dug their foxholes in the Bois Jacques Woods as part of the defense perimeter of Bastogne City that was soon to be surrounded by several enemy divisions. The circumstances were dreadful with constant mortar, rocket and artillery fire, snow fall, temperatures below -28 Celsius at night with little food and ammunition. The field hospital had been captured so little medical help was available. On December 24th the 'E' Company position was attacked at dawn by about 45 enemy soldiers. The attack failed and 'E' Company held their position with 1 casualty against 23 of the enemy. The position of 'E' Company was twice bombed and strafed by American P-47s. During the periods of January 9th and January 13th 'E' Company suffered its most casualties ending with the attack and capture of Foy on January 13th. 8 were killed in Foy and 6 earlier. During the whole period 32 were wounded and 21 were evacuated with cold weather illnesses. In many units involved in the defense of Bastogne the casualties were even greater. This monument is dedicated to all that fought and is symbolic of what happened to other units during the Battle of the Bulge. Airborne Always"

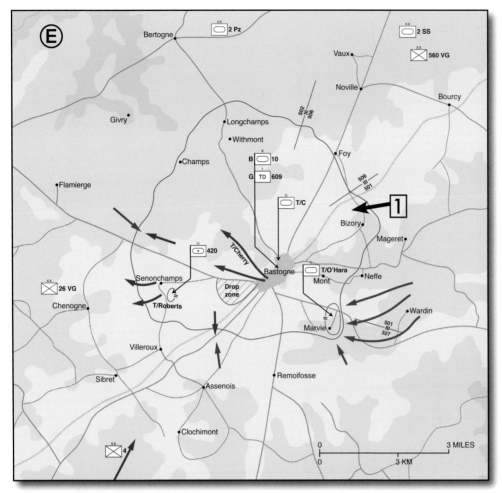

B *There are a number of tank turrets on pedestals around Bastogne. These have moved over the years as is well covered by the STIWOT/Traces of War website. This one—a T23 turret with a 10th Armd patch and a 76mm gun—is on the road to the Mardasson Memorial. The associated panel says:*
"The U.S. 10th Armored Division's Combat Command B, the first major combat unit to defend Bastogne, arrived on the evening of December 18, 1944. Col William L. Roberts deployed his Combat Command in three teams: Team Desobry at Noville, Team Cherry at Neffe and Longvilly, Team O'Hara at Wardin and Marvie.
After delaying the initial German advance, the remnants of these 10th Armored teams joined the 101st Airborne Division for the remainder of the siege. In recognition of their gallant actions, Combat Command B was awarded the Presidential Unit Citation."

D *CC-47A-40-DL 42-24051 of 73rd Troop Carrier Sqn, 434th Troop Carrier Gp, is dropping supplies to the Bastogne defenders. Poor weather and solid cloud cover over the town meant that Pathfinders had to drop to set up Eureka beacons for the C-47s to home in on. Each C-47 carried some 1,200lb of supplies, and on December 23 in just over four hours, 241 planes dropped 144 tons of supplies. Three days later there was a glider drop, ten carrying fuel and one a much-needed surgical team. Throughout the 26th, there were additional resupply sorties. The next day the last of the aerial resupply missions came in two waves. The first had few problems; the second, towing fifty gliders loaded with ammunition, had more difficulty, losing thirteen aircraft and seventeen gliders.*

E *The encirclement of Bastogne. (1) marks the location of the Easy Company memorial.*

F and G *Then and now views of Neffe, where Team Cherry's HQ was set up. This is a January 17 photo, showing an M4A3 of 6th Armd Div knocked out by men from the SdKfz 250.*

127

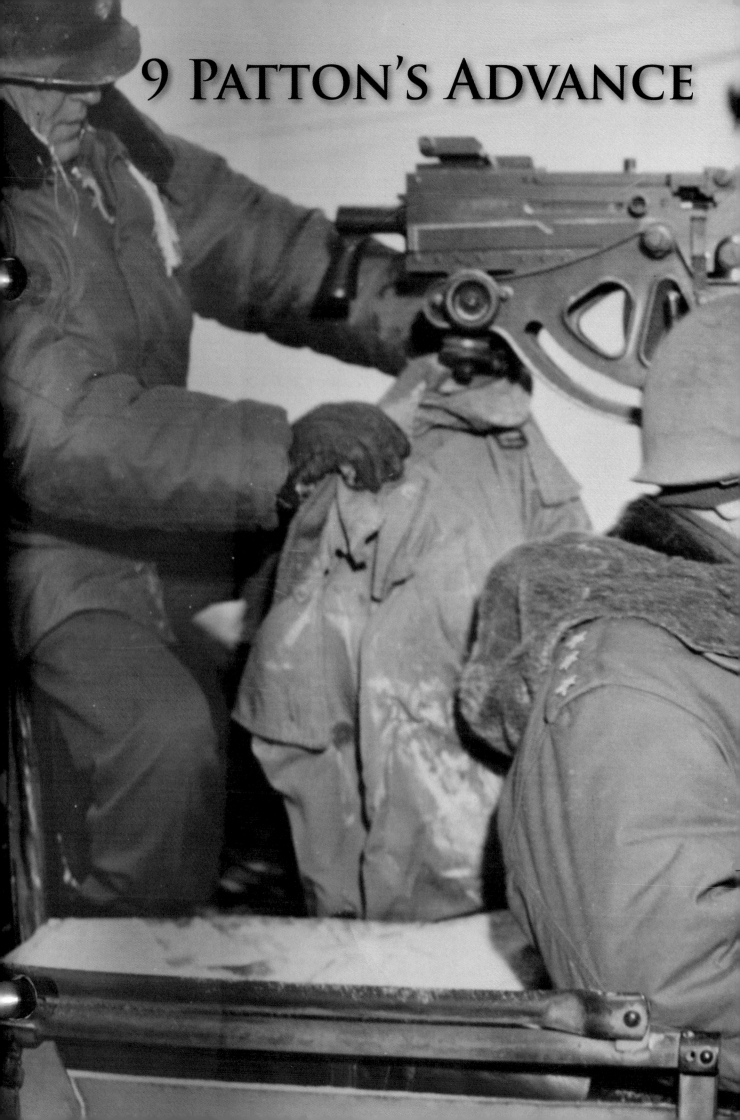

If anyone embodies the cult of the military general as hero, George Patton, Jr does. Foul-mouthed but well-read, a ladies' man with a hard edge Patton courted Press adulation but all too often received condemnation for inopportune outbursts or actions. Today he is often identified as the U.S. Army's "greatest wartime general" although, in reality, Third Army had not had a great deal of hard fighting since becoming operational on August 1 and Patton had not had many opportunities to create the myth that now surrounds him: a chevauchée through France pursuing an exhausted enemy fleeing annihilation in Normandy; tank battles in Lorraine against poorly trained and untested troops, dismissed by Carlo d'Este as "battalions made up of deaf men, others of cooks, and others consisting entirety of soldiers with stomach ulcers"; the protracted siege of the fortress of Metz and coming up against the Westwall in the Saar. Indeed, far from spearheading the Allied attacks, Third Army was peripheral as First Army attacked Aachen on German soil and British forces reached Antwerp and then conducted Operation Market Garden. All this was to change in December 1944.

Patton was preparing his assault on the Saar towards Frankfurt when Oscar Koch, Third Army's intelligence officer (G-2), alerted him to enemy movements in the Ardennes. This was on December 9, and while Patton did not did not halt his planning for the drive to the Rhine, he did more than

Previous Page: Patton's presence bolstered morale and endeared him to the GIs. D'Este noted: "Patton made it a point to be seen during the Bulge, always riding in an open armored jeep. The cold was so intense that most soldiers dressed in as many layers of clothing as they could manage, but Patton's only concession to the glacial temperatures was a heavy winter parka or overcoat."

Opposite, Above: Clearing tree roadblocks on the way to Bastogne. Throughout the campaign, and used by both sides, tree trunks proved an effective method of holding up armor. Much of the Ardennes terrain is steep and heavily wooded and vehicles which could not travel offroad had many problems. Tanks, too, slipped around on icy roads. When 2nd Armd Div moved to Belgium, "Hazardous road conditions due to ice, snow and mud, the adverse weather conditions and the problem of driving at night under complete blackout, made the march very unpleasant ... the Division made a very successful move except for several vehicular casualties due to breakdowns, collisions and slipping-off the icy roads." See also the photo on p. 167.

Opposite, Center: Men of the 10th AIB manning a Browning .30cal light machinegun in a foxhole somewhere in the Bastogne sector, January 3.

Opposite, Below: The gunner on a 4th Armd Div halftrack loads a new belt of .50cal.

Above Left: A classic view of 4th Armd Div in the snow around Bastogne, showing men from an AIB passing a White halftrack.

Bottom Left: Lt Wallace Lippincott on the left in the lead tank, Bavigne, Luxembourg, going up into the Battle of the Bulge, a few days before he was killed. This tank was knocked out two days earlier. Lippincott was awarded the Silver Star for returning to the tank and putting out the fire. He was killed on January 14, 1945, in Sonlez, Luxembourg.

continued on page 138

take note. Planning to tackle this new threat was to go ahead immediately to ensure that, "We'll be in a position to meet whatever happens."

This knowledge didn't stop Patton arguing vehemently with Eisenhower on December 16 when instructed to send 10th Armd Div north to Middleton's VIII Corps, but after meeting Bradley in Luxembourg on the 18th, Patton consigned the Saar offensive to the wastebin and was able to shock Eisenhower at the hastily called meeting at Verdun on December 19 when he said Third Army could be ready to go in three days. "Don't be fatuous, George," Eisenhower said—but it was Georgie's boys that pulled Ike's chestnuts out of the fire, thanks to Koch who went on to become head of the Intelligence Department in the Ground Forces School at Fort Riley.

Third Army's plan looked simple on paper: reorient the entire III Corps, led by the 4th Armd Div, to be followed by the XII Corps, to head north. But, as all those involved in the logistics of this sort of operation identified, it was a difficult maneuver and was brilliantly executed. One interesting aside: Patton was initially unconvinced that Bastogne should be held. It took Bradley and Middleton's arguments to change his mind.

Below right: *From their concentration area 4th Armd Div attacked northward creating a corridor through to Bastogne.*

Opposite, Above left: *On December 26, 1944, the first spearhead units of the Third Army's 4th Armd Div reached Bastogne, opening a corridor for relief and resupply of the besieged forces.*

Opposite, Above right: *There were many heroes during the fighting. Pvt James R. Hendrix of the 53rd AIB, 4th Armd Div, at Assenois, on December 26, 1944, showed repeated heroism. His Medal of Honor citation said, "… he was with the leading element engaged in the final thrust to break through to the besieged garrison at Bastogne when halted by a fierce combination of artillery and small arms fire. He dismounted from his halftrack and advanced against two 88mm guns, and, by the ferocity of his rifle fire, compelled the guncrews to take cover and then to surrender. Later in the attack he again left his vehicle, voluntarily, to aid two wounded soldiers, helpless and exposed to intense machinegun fire. Effectively silencing two hostile machineguns, he held off the enemy by his own fire until the wounded men were evacuated.*

"Pvt Hendrix again distinguished himself when he hastened to the aid of still another soldier who was trapped in a burning halftrack. Braving enemy sniper fire and exploding mines and ammunition in the vehicle, he extricated the wounded man and extinguished his flaming clothing, thereby saving the life of his fellow soldier …" This memorial to Hendrix is at Assenois.

Opposite, Center: *Tanks knocked out or abandoned during the battle are recovered for reuse.*

Opposite, Below: *It's difficult to compare the Panther and the Sherman without getting into angels on pinheads territory. The Panther was larger, as can be seen here, but in the end, the experience and ability of the crew was the crucial factor, as was proved in Lorraine.*

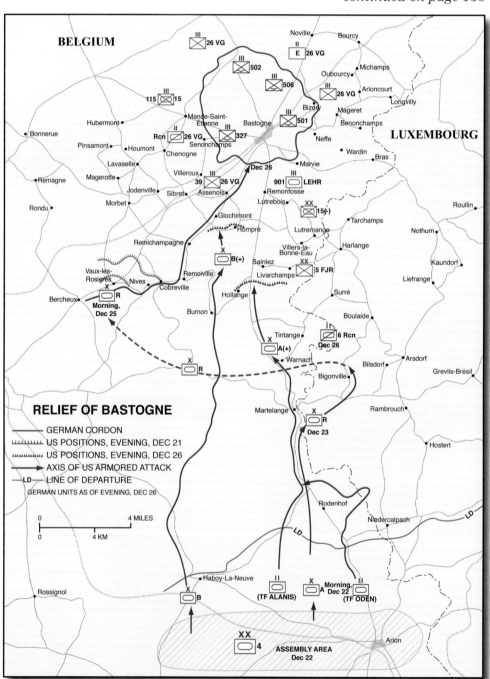

RELIEF OF BASTOGNE

— GERMAN CORDON
⨑⨑⨑ US POSITIONS, EVENING, DEC 21
⨑⨑⨑ US POSITIONS, EVENING, DEC 26
➔ AXIS OF US ARMORED ATTACK
LD— LINE OF DEPARTURE
GERMAN UNITS AS OF EVENING, DEC 26

Above: *Maj Albin F. Irzyk was commander of 8th Tank Bn, 4th Armd Div during World War II. He would serve in the U.S. Army until 1971, reaching the rank of brigadier-general, commanding 14th Armored Cavalry Regiment during the Berlin Crisis of 1961. He was assistant Commander of the 4th Inf Div in South Vietnam and CG Fort Devens, MA. Irzyk was injured during the thrust towards Bastogne when his tank was hit and its turret cracked at Chaumont. Patton's promise of three divisions in forty-eight hours meant that 4th Armd Div had been on the move for more than twenty-two hours before the attack began—traveling over 150 miles under black-out conditions, often without or with only poor maps. Their luck held for the first day of the attack, where there was minimal action.*

PLACE DU GENERAL IRZYK

GENERAL ALBIN F. IRZYK, DSC
Commandant du 8ème Bataillon de Chars Blindés
(4ème Division Blindée – 3ème Armée Américaine)

This Spread: *The advance started with visibility at almost zero, the fields packed with snow, and icy roads. The first main action came after some ten miles, at Burnon where the bridge had been blown. 24th ECB did its duty, and CCB was ordered to stop for the night. The other arms of the attack, CCA and CCR, hadn't made as much progress. Shortly after, the orders were countermanded, "Move all night!" Luckily, again, there was little enemy action, but at Chaumont everything changed. Having moved into the village against slight opposition, the enemy in the form of the Führer Grenadier Brigade, launched an aggressive armored counterattack. Hardly a building in Chaumont was left undamaged. 8th Tank Battalion —when up to strength boasting seventy-six tanks—was badly hit. B Company had a single tank; the other medium tank companies were also badly hit: one had seven left, and the other six. The battalion resumed its march toward Bastogne with only fourteen medium tanks. Chaumont has been rebuilt and Al Irzyk and his men have been remembered as these photos show.*

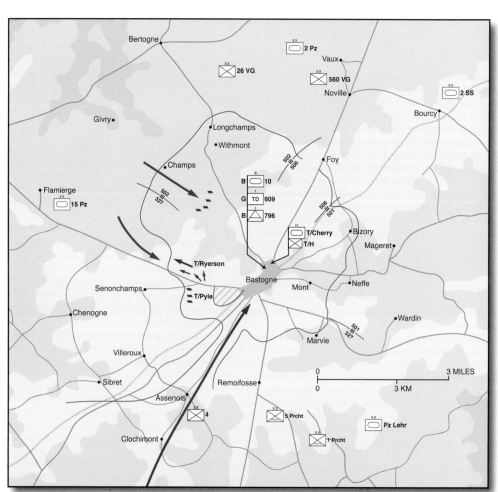

Above: *A 4th Armd Div M5 light tank moves toward Bastogne along the Assenois Road, December 27.*

Above Right: *Elements of Third Army punched through to Bastogne from the southwest. They met the 326th Engineers at around 16:50 on December 26. A day later Gen. Maxwell D. Taylor reached Bastogne with the 4th Armd Div and resumed command of the 101st Airborne. The attacks at Champs and Mont were nowhere near as intensive as the previous day's. The main interest for the defenders was the airdrop of supplies and the arrival, that evening, of the lead tank of 4th Armd Div. The siege had been lifted!*

Center, Left: *Patton's After Action Report illustrates Third Army's attack.*

Center, Right: *The plaque reads: "Near here on the line Longchamps–Monaville in December 1944, the 2nd Bn of 502nd PIR supported by the Antitank/AA Bn of the 101st Airborne courageously defended the Bastogne perimter."*

Right: *Kampfgruppe Maucke attacked and broke through between the 327th GIR and 502nd PIR at Champs on Christmas morning. Hard fighting and help from 705th TD Bn saw them off as this KO'd PzKpfw IV attests.*

Left: *1Lt Charles Boggess, Cpl Milton Dickerman and Pvts James G. Murphy, Hubert S. Smith and Harold Hafner pose on their M4A3E2 Sherman Jumbo Cobra King. They had led the final dash into Bastogne and linked up with the A/326th AB Engr Bn of the 101st Airborne, at a pillbox about two miles from the town center.*

Below Left: *The plaque on this bunker reads: "In memory of Lt Charles P. Boggess (1911–1985) whose tank was the first to break the encirclement of Bastogne. Here, in the evening of December 26, 1944, 4th Armd Div of Patton's Third Army met with 101st Airborne Division thus breaking the encirclement of Bastogne." In March 1945 Cobra King had its 75mm replaced by a 76mm main gun and ended up as a gate guardian for Rose Barracks in Vilseck, Germany. Restoration by the Patton Museum included replacing the original 75mm with one found on another vehicle.*

Bottom Left: *Lt Gen George S. Patton Jr. awards Brig. Gen. Anthony C. McAuliffe the U.S. Army Distinguished Service Cross for his defense of Bastogne. Lt Col Steve Chappuis (not visible) was also awarded a DSC. The ceremony took place at the Chateau Rolle which served as a command post, barracks (for men of 502nd PIR), aid station, kitchen, and weapons depot.*

Below: *The battle around Bastogne didn't stop when the encirclement was broken: immediately after the siege had been lifted, the U.S. forces had to contend with a significant increase in German pressure as they fought to break the narrow corridor into the city. Many other German units became involved, including those elements of 1st SS-Panzer Division* Leibstandarte *still in theater, 9th SS-Panzer Division* Hohenstaufen, *and 12th SS-Panzer Division* Hitlerjugend. *The battle intensified but XLVII Panzerkorps was denied its victory as Third Army moved on northwards to crush the remnants of the attacking force. (See also p. 158.)*

Exactly as promised, at 06:00 on December 22 Patton's attack kicked off, but the roads were no better for his armor than they were for Manteuffel's, and in addition he met the 5th Fallschirmjäger Division of German Seventh Armee along the way. While the German paratroopers were not as tough as earlier in the war, with timely Panzerjäger support they held up the lead columns time and again, forcing the spearhead 4th Armd Div to fight for every inch of its advance. Indeed, critics of Patton—and few are ambivalent about the fiery general—point out that his criticisms of others for being slow to attack can be balanced against committing forces piecemeal and too quickly, and that without the necessary force levels he lost too much time and too many men against Seventh Armee, a far from front-line force.

Be that as it may, on December 26, Lt Col Creighton Abrams, leading 37th Battalion of 4th Armd Div's CCR, finally reached the perimeter, and paused to decide what to do. Bristling German strongpoints were on every side so there was no safe option. But while he stood there Abrams witnessed another desperate airlift of supplies to Bastogne. He decided to simply go hell-bent for the town, and after running a gauntlet of fire, at 16:50 in the afternoon, five Shermans of Company B made it through. The arrival of Third Army tanks was met with jubilation by the defenders of Bastogne—the ring had been broken and they were restored to the U.S. front.

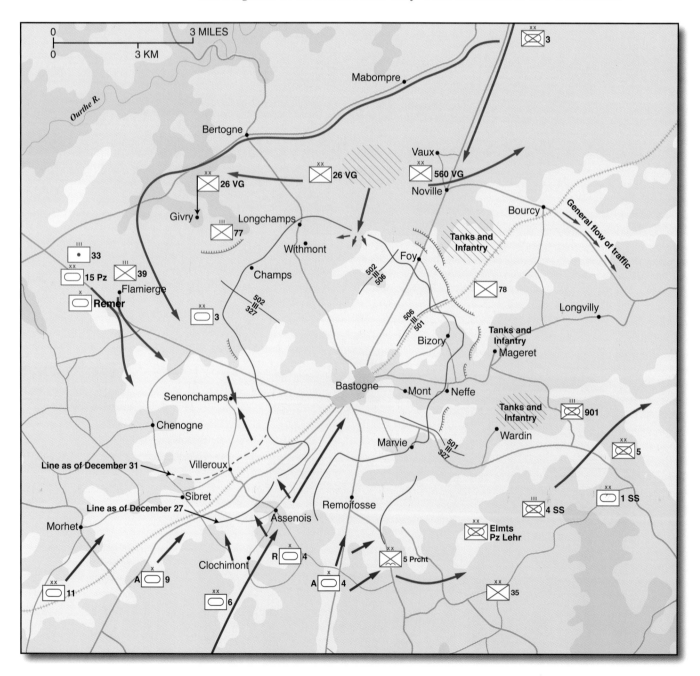

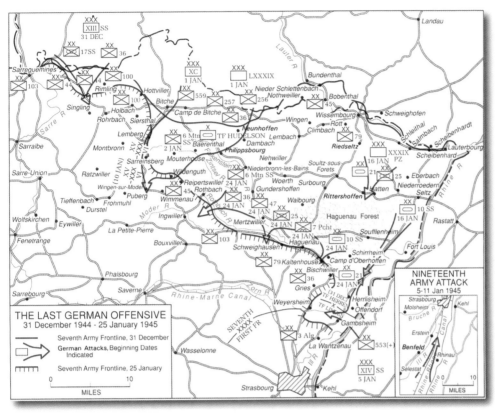

Left: *Operation* Nordwind *was a hard-fought affair overshadowed by what was going on in Belgium and Luxembourg.*
German losses were around 23,000 killed, wounded, or missing. The Seventh Army had 11,609 casualties and 2,836 cases of trench foot, and took 5,985 German prisoners.

Below: *714th Tank Bn moving from Buschwiller to Drusenheim on January 8.*

On that day, too, the 2nd Panzer Division, whose advance elements had come almost within sight of the Meuse, was hammered back from its objective by the U.S. 2nd Armd Div and British 3RTR. During the following days the Germans would pound at Third Army's thin relief corridor to Bastogne, even as Patton's follow-up divisions sought to expand it. But by then the Germans had given up on the initial, grandiose goal of their offensive, and only sought to forestall further Allied offensives. Weeks of vicious attritional fighting would follow; but Patton's arrival at Bastogne had sealed the fate of Hitler's last great gamble in the West.

However, it had also reduced the defenses to the south, and the Germans took advantage of this, launching Operation *Nordwind* (North Wind) in Alsace and Lorraine on December 31. Its goal was to break the U.S. Seventh and French First armies and allow Operation *Zahnarzt* (Dentist) to attack the rear of the Third Army. Seventh Army had taken over much of Third Army's duties as Patton wheeled north, enabling two German army groups, —G under Generaloberst Johannes Blaskowitz and *Oberrhein* (Reichsführer-SS Heinrich Himmler)—to attack the roughly seventy-mile-long front line. At Bitche the attack was held, but at Hatten-Rittershoffen and Herrlisheim Seventh Army struggled to cope with the intense attack, and Eisenhower was forced to send troops to the south to help. However, the line held and the attack ended with the Germans suffering heavy casualties. In turn, this would reduce their capability to defend in the Saar-Palatinate and south Germany.

10 DRIVE TO THE MEUSE

The Meuse at Dinant. Taken on September 5, 1944, by 1st Battalion 39th Inf Regt, the bridge—blown by the Germans—was replaced shortly after. During the Bulge it was one of the German targets and 2nd Panzer got within a few miles of the city before succumbing to fuel shortages and Allied armor attacks.

IN DEDICATION
TO
THE OFFICERS AND MEN OF
TASK FORCE HOGAN
NOW DESIGNATED - 3RD BN 33RD ARMOR ("PICKLES")
3RD ARMORED DIVISION

THE BATTLE OF THE BULGE, 22 DEC 1944. TASK FORCE (TF) HOGAN REPULSED REPEATED ATTACKS
BY OVERWHELMING ENEMY FORCES. LOW ON SUPPLIES, THE GF FOUGHT THROUGH ENEMY LINES FROM HERE TO
MARCOURAY ON 25 DEC. OUT OF FUEL, AMMUNITION AND SURROUNDED BY THREE GERMAN DIVISIONS,
TF HOGAN DESTROYED ITS EQUIPMENT, INFILTRATED ENEMY LINES AND REJOINED 3RD ARMORED DIVISION.

TASK FORCE HOGAN

HQ 3RD BN. 33RD ARMD REGT.   1ST PHAT CO. C. 83RD RCN. BN.
A CO. 33RD ARMD REGT.   A BATTERY, 54 FA BN.
A CO. 83RD RCN BN.   SECTION OF 486TH AAA BN.

Above and Right: *This M4A3(76)W has been sited in Beffe since 1984. With the markings C Coy of 771st Tank Bn, which was attached to 334th Infantry, part of 84th Division, this vehicle did not belong to Task Force Hogan although the plaque is dedicated to the unit. Lt Col Samuel M. Hogan commanded the 3rd Bn of 33rd Inf Regt, 3rd Armd Div. His task force was cut off in the village of Marcouray on the road to La Roche (1 on the map below) for some days before he and his men spiked their weapons and made it back to their own lines on foot.*

Below: *The thrust that got closest to the Meuse came up against the shortened defensive line set up by Montgomery— U.S. XVIII Airborne Corps in the east, U.S. VII Corps in the west, U.S. VIII Corps to the south, and BR XXX Corps on the Meuse.*

With their primary axis of attack, Sixth SS-Panzerarmee's I SS-Panzer Korps, held fast on the northern shoulder, the Fifth Panzer-armee attack towards the Meuse became the key struggle for the Germans as they tried to maintain momentum and the initiative. Heavy fighting ensued around Christmas 1944, with the main battles taking place along the First Army positions between Trois-Ponts and Dinant. Held from west to east by U.S. VII Corps (Collins)—2nd Armored, 84th Infantry, and 3rd Armored divisions—and U.S. XVIII Corps (Ridgway)—7th Armored and 82nd Airborne divisions—the defensive line was attacked by II Panzerkorps of Sixth SS-Panzerarmee, and further west by LVIII and XLVII Panzerkorps of Fifth Panzerarmee. The Germans were running short of fuel but were still a coherent and dangerous enemy, and while their initial strategic concept of Antwerp and splitting the Allied armies was even less realistic now, the offensive continued. LVIII Korps' KG Bayer was beaten back at Hotton on December 21, and 156 PzGr Regt at Marche and Verdenne on December 24–26. At the same time, II SS-Panzerkorps took Baraque Fraiture crossroads on December 23. Manhay and Grandmenil fell shortly after, but were retaken by 3rd Armd Div's Task Force McGeorge on the 26/27th. XLVII Korps' 2nd Pz Div advanced the farthest, reaching Foy-Notre Dame and Celles within a few miles of Dinant. Out of fuel and short of ammo, they were stopped at Foy by British 3RTR and routed at Celles by U.S. 2nd Armd Div. Surrounded, KG Holtmere tried to break them out but were stopped at Custinne on December 25. Panzer Lehr's KG von Poschinger took Rochefort after close-quarters fighting on December 24, but was unable to advance further. The town was retaken within the week. It was, as so many commentators say, "the high tide mark" of the offensive.

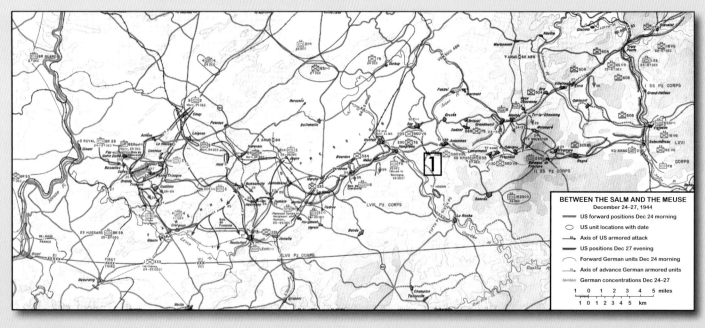

BETWEEN THE SALM AND THE MEUSE
December 24–27, 1944

US forward positions Dec 24 morning
US unit locations with date
Axis of US armored attack
US positions Dec 27 evening
Forward German units Dec 24 morning
Axis of advance German armored units
German concentrations Dec 24–27

1 0 1   2   3   4   5 miles
1 0 1 2 3 4 5 km

Left: *116th Pz Div's KG Bayer had taken Samrée and Dochamps and now moved on Hotton and its bridge over the Ourthe. Held up by stout defense on December 21, the KG turned back to reroute to Marche via Roche without realizing how meager the defenders were. This was a crucial moment in the attack—LVIII Korps would not have a better chance. But the small band of engineers defending the bridge held out.*

Below Left: *Soldiers of the 23rd Engineer Regt attached to 3rd Armd Div guarding a road near Hotton, December 28.*

Below: *Memorial to those who fought around Verdenne. Les Meloures/WikiC/(CC BY-SA 4.0)*

Bottom: *Tank crews from 3rd Armd Div inspect two 116th Pz Div tanks knocked out in Hotton. The partially hidden tank is a PzKpfw IV with a Panther in the foreground.*

Hotton

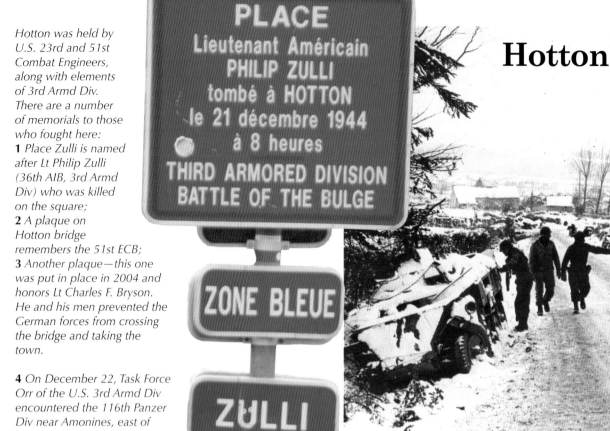

Hotton was held by U.S. 23rd and 51st Combat Engineers, along with elements of 3rd Armd Div. There are a number of memorials to those who fought here:

1 Place Zulli is named after Lt Philip Zulli (36th AIB, 3rd Armd Div) who was killed on the square;

2 A plaque on Hotton bridge remembers the 51st ECB;

3 Another plaque—this one was put in place in 2004 and honors Lt Charles F. Bryson. He and his men prevented the German forces from crossing the bridge and taking the town.

4 On December 22, Task Force Orr of the U.S. 3rd Armd Div encountered the 116th Panzer Div near Amonines, east of Hotton. The knocked-out German SdKfz 251/7 halftracks have been pushed to the side of the road. Held at Hotton, 116th Pz rerouted back through Roche and 560th VG Div took over the attack.

5 Newly arrived on the scene, A and B Coys of 1/517th PIR were ordered to attack from Soy to Hotton to take the high ground and relieve the pressure on Hotton. The fighting was so severe, against fanatical enemy resistance, that the battalion was awarded the Presidential Unit Citation for the action.

PLACE
Lieutenant Américain
PHILIP ZULLI
tombé à HOTTON
le 21 décembre 1944
à 8 heures
THIRD ARMORED DIVISION
BATTLE OF THE BULGE

ZONE BLEUE

ZULLI

1

4

Dedicated To

51st Engineer Combat Battalion
17-23 December 1944

The engineers delayed and stopped elements of the Fifth German Panzer Army along the Ourthe River from Durbuy to LaRoche, defended and held the critical bridge at Hotton in a seven-hour battle on 21 December, fought significant delaying actions at Champlon Crossroads and allowed the Allied defensive lines to be reinforced.

2

3

Melvin E. Biddle
(1923 –2010)

Melvin E. Biddle was a private first class in Coy B of the 1/517th PIR near Soy, Belgium, on 23 and 24 December. His Congressional Medal of Honor citation identifies him as lead scout during the attack to relieve Hotton. At close quarters — within 20 yards of enemy positions—he "killed three snipers with unerring marksmanship. Courageously continuing his advance an additional 200 yards, he discovered a hostile machine-gun position and dispatched its two occupants. He then located the approximate position of a well-concealed enemy machine-gun nest, and crawling forward threw hand grenades which killed two Germans and fatally wounded a third. After signaling his company to advance, he entered a determined line of enemy defense, coolly and delib-erately shifted his position, and shot three more enemy soldiers. Undaunted by enemy fire, he crawled within 20 yards of a machine-gun nest, tossed his last hand grenade into the position, and after the explosion charged the emplacement firing his rifle." During the night, he scouted enemy positions and at daybreak he again led the advance destroying another MG position. Biddle received his medal from the hands of President Truman on October 30, 1945.

Above: *2nd Armd Div mortar team near Amonines.*

Below: *A December view of the bridge over the Ourthe at Hotton. A gentle river in the summer, in winter it is a sizable obstacle.* Jean Housen/ WikiC (CC BY-SA 3.0)

TO SAMRÉE   TO MANHAY   TO BASTOGNE   TO VIELSALM

Parker's Crossroads

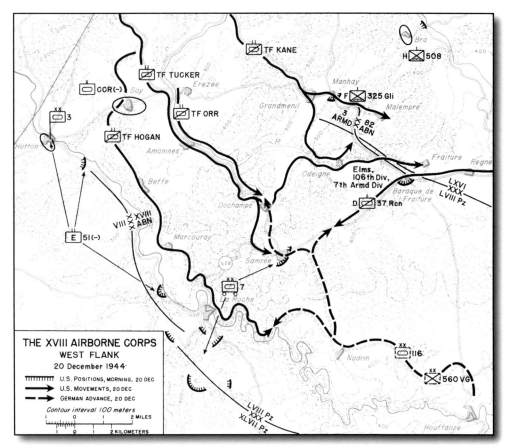

THE XVIII AIRBORNE CORPS
WEST FLANK
20 December 1944

⊓⊓⊓⊓⊓⊓ U.S. POSITIONS, MORNING, 20 DEC
⟶ U.S. MOVEMENTS, 20 DEC
▬ ▬ ▶ GERMAN ADVANCE, 20 DEC

Contour interval 100 meters

Stymied in the north, Sixth SS-Panzerarmee aimed for the Meuse through Manhay. The first step was the crossroads at Baraque Fraiture held by a polyglot collection of units: 589th FA Bn, 106th Inf Div; D Troop, 87th Cav Recon Sqn, 7th Armd Div (M5 Stuarts); D Bty, 203rd AAA Bn, 7th Armd Div; F Coy, 325th GIR, 82nd AB Div; 643rd TD Bn; elements of 3rd Armd Div.

II SS-Panzerkorps' 4th SS-PzGr Regt Der Führer attacked on December 22. The U.S. troops held out until the 23rd and those that could slipped away—three Shermans and forty-four of the 116 men of 325th GIR.

Left: The situation on December 20 before the attack by Der Führer.

Below Left: F Coy, 2/325th GIR heads towards Baraque Fraiture on December 20.

Opposite, Above: This aerial view of the Baraque Fraiture crossroads clearly shows how wooded the area was.

Opposite, Below: Today, the memorial at the crossroads remembers the men who fought here. There's a 105mm M2A1 howitzer and a number of plaques:
A To the American forces who defended the crossroads.
B To all American soldiers. Below, 3rd Armd Div remembers France, Belgium, Germany.
C The crossroads is also known —with a nod, perhaps, to 1862—as Parker's Crossroads after Maj Arthur C. Parker who commanded 589th FA Bn. His unit came to the crossroads from the debacle on the Schnee Eifel.

PANTHER Ausf. **G**
28/12/1944

F # Grandmenil

148

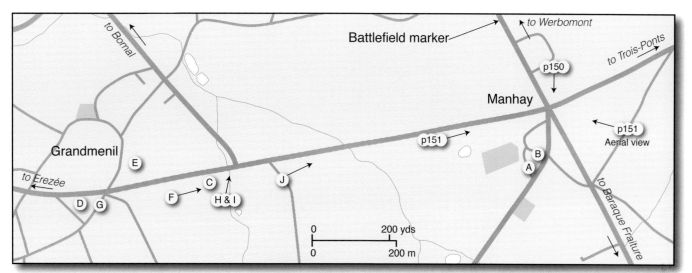

Above: *The area around Manhay, Erezée, and Grandmenil saw intense fighting around Christmas 1944. 7th Armd had taken up positions around Manhay on the 24th. The 2nd SS-Pz Div (Das Reich) attacked late on Christmas Eve. The defenders were deceived by a Judas Goat Sherman leading the enemy column and Manhay was taken. To retake it, 2nd Bn, 424th Inf Regt (of 106th Inf Div) and CCA, 7th Armd, attacked but were badly mauled. The fighting spread to Grandmenil. In the end, 3rd Bn, 517th PIR retook the village on the 27th. The map shows photo locations.*

A *Memorial to 325th GIR, 82nd Airborne.*

B *A German 75mm PaK 40 found in the area.*

C *Memorial to the 951st FA Bn.*

D *Memorial to 75th Inf and 3rd Armd Divs.*

E Das Reich *lost a number of Panthers in the heavy fighting around Manhay. Seven were left around the Bomal–Manhay–Grandmenil area, some destroyed, others out of fuel and more bogged in marshy ground. 407, its suspension damaged and missing its muzzle-brake, today is a memorial at Grandmenil crossroads.*

F *Overview of the road from Grandmenil to Manhay. There are seven Panthers in the fields. In the center is the road junction shown in H and I.*

G *Memorial to 231st ECB.*

H and I *Grandmenil December 30, 1944. A* Das Reich *Panther destroyed by 3rd Bn, 289th Inf Regt, 75th Inf Div lies in front of a wrecked house. The road signs have been twisted.*

J *This Panther threw a track reversing towards Manhay.*

Manhay

This spread: *The crossroads at Manhay after its recapture by U.S. troops. Note the Panther on its side (***Below and Below Right***). Helped by the fact that Manhay fell on the boundary between Ridgway's XVIII AB and Collins' VII Corps, SS-Brigadeführer Heinz Lammerding's 2nd SS-Panzer Division Das Reich swept through the area. U.S. reinforcements came in the form of CCB of 3rd Armd Division, 325th GIR, and—more importantly—artillery units who pounded the area as can be seen from the state of the crossroads in the photo above. Das Reich pulled back on the 27th, but on the 28th KG Krag attacked towards Erezée through Sadzot. The attack was blunted by 509th PIR, but at some cost.*

Above: *Aerial view of the Manhay crossroads.*

Right: *M4s destroyed by SS-Hauptsturmführer Pohl's 4/SS-Panzer-Regt-2 in the attack on Manhay.*

Below: *Memorial at Sadzot remembering the determined U.S. resistance to the attack by 2nd SS-Panzer Division on December 27–28.*

Bottom: *Looking back toward the Manhay crossroads, a heavily camouflaged 3rd Armd Div Sherman keeps watch on the road to Grandmenil.*

The closest the German attack came to the Meuse was around December 24, when elements of 2nd Pz Div were about five miles from the Meuse close to Dinant. But the wheels were coming off the offensive. Bastogne still hadn't fallen and Patton's Third Army was rolling northward. 2nd Pz Div, which had been slowed in battles around Bastogne, ran out of fuel at Celles and was destroyed by U.S. 2nd Armd and British 29th Armd Bde.

Above Right: A PzKpfw IV and a Panther from 2nd Panzer Div's KG von Cochenhausen knocked out in the fighting at Celles.

Center Right: The spearhead of XLVII Panzerkorps' thrust was two Kampfgruppen from 2nd SS-Panzer Division, KG von Böhm and KG von Cochenhausen. The former reached Achêne late on December 23. This KG was reinforced when KG von Cochenhausen reached Celles. There they ran into British 3RTR patrols and CCB of the U.S. 2nd Armd Div who had marched down from Maastricht as part of Montgomery's plan to use Collins' VII Corps to counterattack Fifth Panzerarmee. CCA 2nd Armd Div was further east, attacking Panzer Lehr at Rochefort and Humain on the 24th, cutting off the advanced Kampfgruppen.

Right: Infantrymen of Easy Company, 2nd Bn, 41st Regt, 2nd Armd Div advance to hold newly gained positions in the attack on Humain.

Below: Panthers knocked out at Humain.

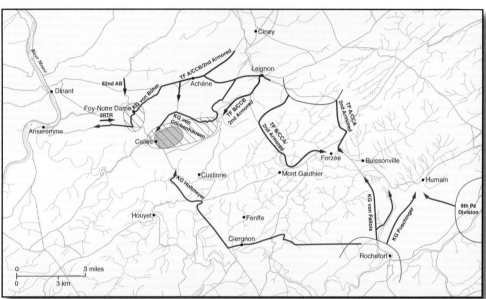

Left: *9th Panzer Division Panther in Humain. A three-day battle was fought out between CCA U.S. 2nd Armd Div and 4th Cavalry Group on the one hand and, on the German side, Panzer Lehr, (later replaced by 9th Pz Div transferred from the Netherlands), as they desperately tried to cut through the U.S. forces to relieve their stranded compatriots. 2nd Armd Div's accurate artillery fire, Allied air support, and finally flame-throwing Crocodile tanks of the Scottish Fife and Forfar Yeomanry, ended the battle.*

Left and Above: *75th Inf Div mop up after the advance of CCA of 2nd Armd Div. This is Forzée ten miles east of Celles on December 26. By this time all hope of relieving the two Kampfgruppen had passed. KG von Böhm had been silenced by 3RTR and KG von Cochenhausen by 2nd Armd Div. The panzers had run out of fuel and the vain attempts to relieve them had been harried by Allied artillery and airpower—the last by KG Holtmeyer which reached Custinne—before U.S. 2nd Armd Div halted them.*

Opposite, Left and Center Left: *The bridge at Dinant flooded by refugees heading west away from the fighting. Montgomery moved British XXX Corps to cover the Meuse bridges. Dinant was covered by British 29th Armoured Brigade with 3RTR providing the patrols over the river.*

Opposite, Below: *A British Sherman Firefly patrols the Meuse at Namur.*

Right: *In Foy-Notre Dame, the farthest extent of 2nd Panzer Division's advance is recorded by one of twenty-six battlefield markers erected by the Touring Club de Belgique (see also p. 189).*

Below: *Today, a Panther marks the high-water mark of the Battle of the Bulge—or the "von Rundstedt Offensive" as it is signed—in Celles.*

CELLES

ICI FUT ARRETEE L'OFFENSIVE VON RUNDSTEDT LE 24 DECEMBRE 1944

BATTLE OF THE BULGE

A CELLES, en décembre 1944, lors de la Bataille des Ardennes, l' avance allemande fut définitivement stoppée grâce à l' assaut victorieux de la 2nd Armored Division US et du 3th Royal Tank Regiment UK

11 THE ALLIED COUNTERATTACK

In honor of the gallant soldiers
of the 2nd and 3rd US Armored Divisions
who liberated our town and its villages
in January 1945 during the Battle of the Bulge.

M4A1 SHERMAN TANK (76-mm. gun),
restored and put in position by the Belgian
"1/3 Régiment de lanciers" (Cavalry Regiment)

La Roche-en-Ardenne, 17th December 2004

Previous Page: *U.S. M4A1(76) in La Roche-en-Ardenne. Until 2004 this position had been taken by an M26 Pershing but this vehicle was deemed more representative.*

Below Right: *Another armored memorial at La Roche. The plaque reads: "Honour and tribute to the 1st Northamptonshire Yeomanry who supported the 51st Highland Division in the liberation of La Roche on 11th January 1945." It is an Achilles, a British M10 TD armed with a QF 17-pdr in place of the standard 3-inch M7 gun.*

Below: *Infantry of the 2nd Monmouthshire Regt, 53rd (Welsh) Division, in the snow near Hotton, January 4, 1945. Note the PIAT and Bren.*

Opposite, Above left and right: *Fireflies of B Sqn East Riding Yeomanry, part of 33rd Armd Bde, lining the western bank of the Ourthe in Hotton on January 4—and the same view today. The 33rd Armd Bde first supported 53rd Welsh Div, then the advance of the 51st Highland Div.*

Opposite, Center right: *Memorial at Hotton, a Firefly turret with a plaque, "In tribute to the gallant soldiers of the 53rd (Welsh) Inf Div and their attached armoured regiments who liberated our towns and villages in January 45 during the Ardennes Offensive."*

Opposite, Below: *Churchills waiting to move forward to support British 53rd Inf Div. British troops were withdrawn on January 16.*

Following the failure to cross the Meuse, the end of December saw the Germans turn their attention to Bastogne. Manteuffel attacked the corridor opened by Third Army from the northwest and southeast. At Sibret on December 30, the Führer Begleit Brigade and 3rd PzGr Div made initial successes, taking Chenogne, before 11th Armd Div halted the attack. At the same time, elements of *Leibstandarte*, *Panzer Lehr*, and 5th FJR, along with 167th VG Div, attacked towards Lutrebois. They were devastated by 4th Armd Div's artillery, XIX TAC's fighter-bombers, and the tanks and TDs of 4th Armd Div and 654th TD Bn.

Thus, only two weeks after the German offensive began, with reinforcements rushing to the area, on January 3 the Allies went fully on the offensive themselves as First and Third armies headed towards a linkup at Houffalize, with British XXX Corps—as the map on page 159 shows—attacking from the west.

As with all facets of the Allied campaigns against Germany there are debates about aspects of the counter-attack—how long it took to set up and the ambition of its intent. As is often the case in these matters, there's no clear-cut right or wrong, and much of the debate is promoted by the Montgomery-knockers. Fact is, that the weather at the start of 1945 was awful. It was frighteningly cold, leaving roads icy and difficult to negotiate. Carlo d'Este sums it up graphically: "everyone suffered in temperatures that

dropped off the thermometer ... Freezing fog again grounded the air forces ... a gain of two miles a day was considered a great accomplishment." Unsurprising, therefore, that he describes the counter-attack as moving sluggishly. It's ten miles from Bastogne to Houffalize: First and Third armies linked up on January 16, thirteen days after the attack began. During that period, Allied tactical air forces were only able to operate on three of the days. In the south, Patton's spearheads—11th and 6th Armored divisions made slow progress. In the north, II Panzerkorps—comprising 2nd SS-Panzer Division and 12th and 560th VG divisions—fought a tenacious rearguard action. It's hard to see how starting the counterattack earlier would have made much difference, and there is something to said for having allowed more forces to get in position to be involved. On January 7, finally reading the writing on the wall, Hitler gave permission for his troops to withdraw—not as Manteuffel had suggested on the evening of the 24th, to leave the salient completely, but back to a line from La Roche to Longchamps. A week later, he agreed another withdrawal. Still short of fuel, the Germans evaded their pursuers, but it was a fighting withdrawal. It would not be until the end of January that the bulge was finally obliterated.

Above and Above Right: *Cult of the personality. The flamboyant general has memorials all over Luxembourg and Belgium. This one is in Ettelbrück near Diekirch. The main square in the town is also named after him and there is a Patton Museum, too, all grist to the tourism mill. The M4A1 is part of the memorial on the outskirts of town. It is in the colors of HQ Coy, 34th Tank Bn, 5th Armd Div, and has the fittings to take a dozer blade.*

Right: *Liberty Road memorial, Huldange. La voie de la Liberté owes its existence to Guy de la Vasselais, French liaison officer to George S. Patton. Opened on September 17, 1947, it starts on the Cotentin peninsula at Sainte-Mère-Église (the first with a direct reference to Patton is at Camp Patton at Néhou), and travels 1,145km (711 miles).*

Opposite, Below: *4.5-inch M1 field gun "Bitchbuster" of 90th Inf Div at Wilwerdange near Troisvierges on January 27.*

Above: *CEBA memorial at Berlé, Luxembourg. 35th Inf Div's* After Action Report *says of the attack of January 9, "By dark BERLE and 80 PoWs were captured including the Battalion CP of 929th Bicycle Battalion."*

Above Left: *An abandoned PzKpfw VI ausf B (SdKfz 182) Tiger II or Königstiger (known as a King Tiger, in fact zoologically it translates as Bengal Tiger) of sPzAbt 506, Sixth Panzer-armee, is inspected by men of the 137th Inf Regt, 35th Inf Div after it was destroyed by the retreating crew. The 506th was the only Heer (Regular Army) unit equipped with the Tiger II, the others being Waffen SS. On January 17, as the Sixth Panzerarmee retreated from Bastogne, the 506th was forced to abandon two Tiger IIs and one Tiger I.*

Center left: *On January 8, 90th Inf Div, the "Tough Ombres," moved north from the Saar to the Bastogne front. Precautions had been taken to ensure surprise, the* After Action Report *says, "The 94th Infantry Division took over and maintained the 90th's radio traffic in the old area ... Unit markings on personnel and vehicles were covered during the move, a large part of which was made at night ... the Division moved into concealed assembly areas without taking over any part of the front and planned to launch its attack through a portion of the front held by the 26th Division." The security worked well. A directive issued by FJR13 on January 10 said, "It is imperative that steps be taken to ascertain whether or not the American 90th Inf Div has been committed. Special attention must be given to the numbers 357, 358, 359, 343, 344, 345, 915 and 315 [90th's regiment numbers]. Prisoners identified with these numbers will immediately be taken to the Regimental Section." The attack was prosecuted successfully although progress was slow. Photo shows Lt Wallace Lippincott in the lead tank at Bavigne, Luxembourg, heading up to Bastogne. This tank was knocked out and Lippincott was awarded the Silver Star for returning to the tank and putting out the fire. He was killed a few days later, on January 14, in Sonlez.*

161

Above: *Maj Gen Robert W. Grow commanded the "Super Sixth." 6th Armd Div received orders to move north from the Saar on December 23. By the 26th it had been replaced by the 103rd Inf Div. It moved via Metz to Ettelbrück but was subsequently moved to Bastogne, relieving 10th Armd Div. With the 4th Armd Div—who had spearheaded the relief of Bastogne—placed in III Corps reserve. After three days of attacking, little ground had been made. The 6th was pulled back to better positions but lost a number of men in the withdrawal. Powerful German attacks over the next days were broken up by artillery fire. On the 10th 4th Armd Div returned to the front and on the 12th the Germans started pulling out. By the 15th, 6th Armd Div were at Arloncourt; by the 23rd Troisvierges; by the 26th they closed on the River Our and the German border. Robert Grow had a checkered career. In 1952, when a military attaché in Moscow, he was court-martialed after portions of his diary were copied by an alleged Soviet agent and published. In the frenzied anti-Communist atmosphere of the United States in the early 1950s, this became a media sensation and led to a questionable trial led by Grow's erstwhile colleague, Lt Gen Maxwell D. Taylor.*

Opposite, Above: *6th Armd Div, as George Hofmann writes in* The Super Sixth, *"entered the Battle of the Bulge by completing the relief of the 10th Armd Div" on December 26. Moving to Bastogne on the 28th, on New Year's Eve the division attacked through Bizory (as seen here), Mageret, and Neffe. Heavy fighting and repeated German counterattacks were blunted by remarkable firepower from Div Arty who fired 53,045 rounds between January 1 and 7. This aerial view of Bizory shows 6th Armd Div on January 13.*

Opposite, Center: *Memorial in honor of the 6th Armd Div's role in the Battle of the Bulge in Heinerscheid.* Les Meloures/ WikiCommons (CC BY-SA 3.0)

Opposite, Below: *The Super Sixth's path through Europe.*

Above Left: *Hofmann talks of how the men of 6th Armd Div learned a trick from the Germans: "white camouflage. Every house in Bastogne was checked for white sheets ... Before long vehicles were draped in white and the men covered in white sheets."*

Center Left: *4th Armd Div M4A3 (76mm) covering highway H4 near Bastogne.*

Below: *44th AIB, 6th Armd Div, outside Mageret on January 20.*

Right: *Tiger II of SS-sPzAbt 501 knocked out at Wardin on January 12. The battle for the village was a difficult one. It was cleared by 9th AIB. The Tiger tanks, Hofmann records, "seemed to fly over the snow" unlike the M4s with smaller tracks. Their rounds lack penetration, too, and "bounced off the Tigers like marbles off a brick."*

Below and Bottom: *Two views of 44th AIB, 6th Armd Div, during the attack. The 44th was commanded by Lt Col Charles E. Brown.*

Left: *6th Armd Div Sherman knocked out in the fighting for Mageret, east of Bastogne, on January 1.*

Below: *M4 (105mm howitzer), tank No. 16 of HQ Company, 15th Tank Battalion (Lt Col Embry D. Lagrew), 6th Armd Div. The tankers struggle to keep warm—a perennial problem in January 1945.*

Bottom: *M4A3 Sherman named Caballero of 69th Tank Battalion (Lt Col Chester E. Kennedy), 6th Armd Div, knocked out near Longvilly in late January. A hit can be seen to the immediate left of the vehicle name on the side.*

Above: *A 2nd Armd Div column led by an M36 TD makes its way toward Dochamps. On January 3, 1945, 2nd Armd Div launched an attack from near Hotton in deep snow. Its mission was to clear enemy strongpoints to the Ourthe River near Houffalize. At 10:30 on January 6 CCB attacked toward Dochamps but stubborn enemy resistance stopped the advance about one half mile from the village. Traffic conditions were so bad, that tank companies replaced all steel tracks with rubber. CCA continued the attack at 08:30, January 7, and Dochamps fell late the next day.*

Left: *Tank column at Fisenne near Erezée.*

Above Right: *An overturned M36 of the 702nd TD Bn on the roadside at Fisenne. Two crew members were killed in the incident. The battalion* After Action Report *talks about the thrust south and how "The enemy defended the attack on his flank by numerous counter-attacks and by holding stubbornly from well-concealed positions at all critical points, utilizing artillery and mortar fire, automatic weapons, small arms and bazookas."*

Right: *7th Armd Div in Deidenberg.*

Hitler, on January 14, allowed a further withdrawal; consequently the roads around Aschouffe, and Houffalize became a bottleneck. 116th Panzer Division just managed to escape the pincers that joined at Houffalize. An important crossroads, it had been heavily bombed on the night of January 5–6 to stop German supply columns and the escape route for German forces. As the Allies entered the town, they found it devastated.

Right: *SdKfz 260 abandoned at Houffalize.*

Below Right: *Tanks and other vehicles had little answer to the power and accuracy of Ninth Air Force and U.S. artillery.*

Below: *Two Flakpanzer IV Wirbelwind knocked out— possibly by aircraft cannon fire—near Houffalize.*

Opposite, Above: *Members of the 24th Car Reconnaissance, First Army, greet soldiers from the 507th PIR on January 14, at La Roche-en-Ardenne.*

Opposite, Center: *84th Inf Div of First Army meets 11th Armd Div of Third Army in Houffalize on January 16.*

Opposite, Below: *Another meeting between 11th Armd Div and 84th Inf Div.*

Houffalize

Above: *Plaques on a rock face above the Ourthe remember the meeting of First Army—in the shape of 84th Inf Div and Third Army (11th Armd Div), on January 16. There are three parts: the top plaque illustrates the meeting; the other two give French and English versions of: "Here on 16 Jan 1945 the Bulge was wiped out by the junction of the 84th. Inf. Div. and the 11th. AD."*

Below: *This stele in Houffalize remembers the linkup on January 16.*

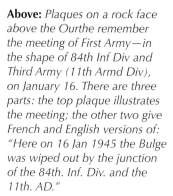

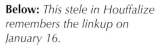

Above and Above Right:
Jagdpanzer IV/70 knocked out in heavy fighting with 3rd Armd Div near Chérain, January 20.

Below Right: *15cm sFH18 in Chérain. Nicknamed "Evergreen," when mounted on a PzKpfw IV chassis it was named Hummel.*

Below: *On December 22, Monty had told Maj-Gen Hasbrouck, CG 7th Armd Div and the units defending St. Vith: "You have accomplished your mission—a mission well-done. It is time to withdraw." It must have been with enormous satisfaction that the same division spearheaded the retaking of the town. The 7th Armd Div After Action Report states baldly: "On 20 January, an attack was launched against ST. VITH from the north. The towns of DEIDENBERG, BORN, and HUNNINGEN were taken successively in the course of the drive and ST. VITH was re-entered on 23 January."*

The tanks of 31st Tank Battalion and the infantry of 48th AIB and of the 509th PIR and a company of 517th PIR (attached to 7th Armd Div for the retaking of St. Vith) were divided into task forces and with no nonsense the 7th Armd Div retook St. Vith, withstood two counterattacks, and moved on. Here (right) paratroopers of the 509th PIR pass a 7th Armd Div M5 near St. Vith. Note the white paint. The After Action Report mentions, "A Camouflage Team from the First U.S. Army visited the division's tank battalions on 5 January to give technical advice and assist in camouflaging the vehicles. On 10 January, the division became the first unit in the First U.S. Army to paint its tanks white for camouflage."

Left, Below Left, and Below: *87th Inf Div was part of SHAEF reserve, until it saw action on December 29. It captured Moircy on December 30, Remagne on the 31st, Gérimont on January 2, and Tillet on January 10. Here, troops of the 87th move up the main street of Bihain, to attack German troops dug in the woods beyond the town.*

Bottom: *Tiger I turret number 411 knocked out on January 15 near Oberwampach east of Bastogne. It comes from sPz-Kompanie "Hummel" which became sPzAbt 506's IV. Kompanie on December 18. Hummel employed the only Tiger Is in the Ardennes.*

Right: *A 75mm PaK 40 gun overlooking Mabompre, just south of Houffalize. This gun has been credited with knocking out two American tanks before it was destroyed.*

Below: *South of Langlir, an M36 TD of 703rd Tank Battalion, 3rd Armd Div, moves past a disabled PzKpfw IV of 115th Panzer Battalion, 15th PzGr Division. The village was captured by 83rd Inf Div on January 12.*

Bottom: *On 6 January, the 80th Division launched an attack across the Sure River and seized Goesdorf and Dahl, Luxembourg. Here, on January 10 a Panzer IV of Führer-Grenadier-Brigade.*

Left: *Civilians had a hard time of it. Opposite Clervaux's GI memorial (see p. 53) is this plaque remembering the liberation.*

Below Left: *A different city, but a similar scene—civilians of Wiltz in Luxembourg at the window of the hospital, watch as their national flag flies again after the town's liberation by 4th Armd Div on December 25.*

Below: *Weilerbach outside Echternach was where 5th Inf Div attacked across the River Sure—the border between Luxembourg and Germany—on February 7, 1945. This memorial remembers the event. The Bulge was well and truly over.*

173

12 DENOUEMENT

When available through the weather breaks, the close support of XIX Tactical Air Force was invaluable to Third Army. Panther near the road between Marnach and Dasburg.

The Battle of the Bulge was one of the greatest tests the U.S. Army faced in World War II, and developed into one of its largest ever battles. A successful deception operation meant that German forces achieved almost complete surprise, and within a week had punched through U.S. First Army's lines, blowing away the 106th Infantry, and advanced to within touching distance of the Meuse. It had caused if not panic, then certainly extreme concern among the Allied command, so much so that Eisenhower passed over control of the northern half of the battlefield to the safe hands of FM Montgomery. His decisive action ensured that 7th Armd Div and other forces around St. Vith were not sacrificed unnecessarily, and the subsequent rearrangement of the defensive line held firm as the German *Schwerpunkt* passed from the Sixth SS-Panzerarmee to Fifth Panzerarmee.

Significant as these actions were, however, the German attack had been derailed by then anyway. The swift Allied response committed their reserves—the veteran 82nd and 101st Airborne Divisions—to the fray and moved 7th Armd Div and others onto the battlefield. The critical battles on the northern shoulder of the Bulge—along the Elsenborn Ridge and the rivers Amblève and Salm—had seen the top German troops, I SS-Panzerkorps, halted. Worse was to follow for them as KG Peiper was not just stopped in its tracks by the bravery of small teams of combat engineers who took away the bridges it needed to advance, but then destroyed by 82nd Airborne and 3rd Armored divisions. Out of fuel, surrounded and bombarded by incessant accurate artillery, Peiper left his tanks—including six of the huge Tiger IIs— and scurried away. II SS-Panzerkorps moved south, was put under Fifth Panzerarmee, and advanced further than I SS-Panzerkorps, before being held by the rearranged line of U.S. XVIII (Airborne), V, and VII Corps.

The success of the German central thrust was mitigated by the holding actions of the 28th Inf Div and what remained of the 106th. Their timetable smashed, von Manteuffel's men had to expend so much time on the way to St. Vith that 7th Armd Div was there to hold them off for long enough to organise the defense behind. Further south, the same was true. The defense of Clervaux and Wiltz meant that 101st Airborne was able to squeeze into Bastogne, joining 9th and 10th Armored divisions before it was surrounded.

And what a defense! Holding the German offensive at bay, Bastogne held out until Patton's Third Army, wheeled from its position on the Saar, relieved it. The fighting intensified as Hitler ordered Bastogne taken and moved whatever forces were left to cut Third Army's corridor, but by January 7 even he had to recognize that the game was up: less than a week later First and Third armies met at Houffalize; two weeks after that the Germans were flooding back into Germany.

There's no doubt that the praise heaped on the United States' forces for their victory was well-earned: they held off a powerful attack that caught them by surprise, and then threw the enemy back. In spite of their own manpower problems, they concentrated greater numbers of men and vehicles into the area, and were able to supply them with fuel, ammunition, and food.

However, the German attack was not as strong as it might have been, prosecuted by divisions that were at less than full strength—Panzer Lehr had only forty percent of its tanks, sixty percent of its guns, and sixty percent of its authorized strength; the 26th VG Div lacked a regiment; 2nd Pz Div was at eighty percent strength, but one of its regiments of grenadiers was on bicycles and was used only for replacements. Units that later reinforced XLVII Panzerkorps ranged in strength from fifty to seventy percent. They lacked sufficient bridging equipment, were chronically short of fuel and ammunition, and resupply was impaired by the traffic jams and the weather.

When the weather cleared, the Allied tactical airforces roamed the skies smashing armor, vehicles, troop concentrations, and—once the German retreat started—the choke points along the narrow, muddy, often steep roads and tracks of Belgium and Luxembourg. In the end, what is most surprising, perhaps, is not that the German attack failed, but that it took place at all.

Loss of equipment

Armor losses were significant for both sides in the Battle of the Bulge. It's usually assessed at around 700–800 U.S. tanks (Eisenhower gave the figure as 733) and the same for the Germans. There is, it is true, a slightly different system of reporting, in that the German losses only included total losses, whereas Allied losses tend to cover those vehicles that were lost to their unit and may have been recovered. Also, the German systems in January 1945 were not as efficient as they had been—the *OKW War Diary*, for example, records the loss of only 222 tanks (77 Mk IV, 132 Mk V, 13 Mk VI) and 102 assault guns for December 16–31, but reporting of December's losses would not always have filtered through until January or later. Many of the German losses were caused by lack of fuel or mechanical problems—for example those of Peiper's *Kampfgruppe*—so it is also difficult to produce a straightforward battle loss figure for either side.

Suffice it to say that on the German side the tank and assault gun losses were close to half those employed in the Ardennes. This represents a very serious loss when one considers (as Cole identifies) that the Western Front received 60% of the new AFV production in November and December (2,277 as against 919) and that the Eastern Front had been denuded of tanks to such an extent that it had only two-thirds of the number employed in the Ardennes as at January 5. Unsurprisingly, when the Russians launched their Vistula-Oder Offensive on January 12, they had a 6:1 advantage in tanks.

1 Wreckage of Führer-Grenadier-Brigade SPWs at Heiderscheid after the battle with 80th Div's 319th Regt on December 23.

2 Jagdpanzer IV destroyed by XIX TAC near Marnach late January.

3 Another Panther KO'd in the retreat.

4 and 5 PzKpfw IVs knocked out by an air attack.

6 Jagdpanzer IV near the road between Marnach and Dasburg.

Casualties

Care of battle casualties is essential for any army and morale suffers if evacuation isn't quick and aid isn't good. U.S. medical services in World War II had improved considerably since the Great War. On June 6, 1944, ETO medical personnel— doctor, dentists, nurses, veterinarians, therapists etc—totaled 132,705, of whom 62,000 were with combat forces. That figure had risen to 245,387 by the end of the war. It was a dangerous job. The Medical Department's field forces had 13,174 casualties of its own—and 2,274 of them were killed. By the end of the war five ETO medics had been awarded the Medal of Honor.

On the frontline treatment tended to be a shot of morphine to prevent shock, sulfa powder to stop infection, and bandage to stop the bleeding. Next, stretchers took patients to a battalion aid station. Seriously injured men could be transported to a collecting station and sent to a portable surgical hospital, a clearing station or an evacuation hospital. From there, the seriously wounded were shipped to a general hospital. The mortality rate of wounded soldiers dropped from 8.1% in World War I to just 3% in World War II.

"Some thirty-two U.S. divisions fought in the Ardennes, where the daily battle strength of U.S. Army forces averaged twenty-six divisions and 610,000 men ... the cost of victory was staggering. The final tally for the Ardennes totaled 41,315 casualties in December to bring the offensive to a halt and an additional 39,672 casualties in January to retake lost ground. The SHAEF casualty estimate presented to Eisenhower in February 1945 listed casualties for the First Army at 39,957; for the Third Army at 35,525; and for the British XXX Corps, which helped at the end, at 1,408 ... Sickness and cold weather also ravaged the fighting lines, with the First, Third, and Seventh (in Alsace) Armies having cold injury hospital admissions of more than 17,000 during the entire campaign. No official German losses for the Ardennes have been computed, but they have been estimated at between 81,000 and 103,000."
From "Ardennes-Alsace", CMH Pub 72-26

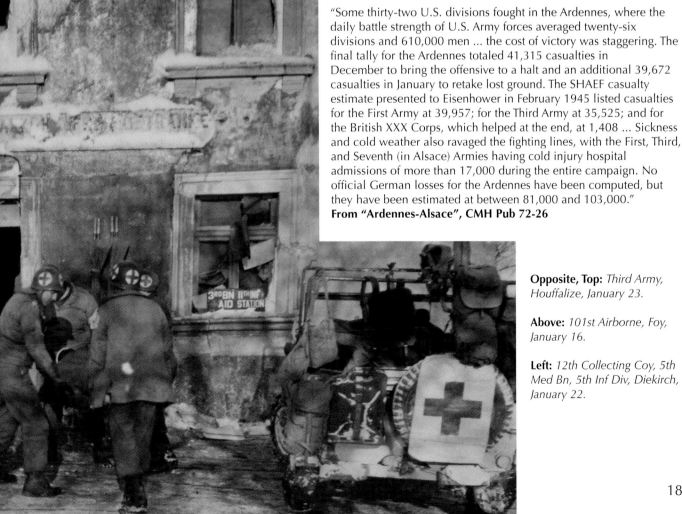

Opposite, Top: *Third Army, Houffalize, January 23.*

Above: *101st Airborne, Foy, January 16.*

Left: *12th Collecting Coy, 5th Med Bn, 5th Inf Div, Diekirch, January 22.*

13 Remembrance

Netherlands American Cemetery and Memorial

The only American military cemetery in the Netherlands is sited at Margraten, some ten miles east of Maastricht. Dominated by a tall memorial tower, the cemetery is 65.5 acres in area, divided into sixteen plots, where rest 8,301 of the dead, their headstones set in long curves. On the Tablets of the Missing are recorded 1,722 names. Rosettes mark the names of those since recovered and identified. The cemetery was established on November 10, 1944, by U.S. Ninth Army. Today, as with all such establishments, it is run by the American Battle Monuments Commission.

Unique to the cemetery, since 1945 members of the local community have adopted the grave sites. They bring flowers to the cemetery and research the life of the service member as a way to honor their sacrifice.

Luxembourg American Cemetery and Memorial

The Luxembourg American Cemetery and Memorial was established on December 29, 1944, by the 609th QM Company of U.S. Third Army. It's 50.5 acres in area. Lt Gen George S. Patton was buried here after his death following an auto accident—he wanted to be buried among his men. He had moved his headquarters to Luxembourg City on December 28. Not far from the cemetery entrance stands a white stone chapel (above left), with sculpture in bronze and stone, a stained glass window with American unit insignia, and a mosaic ceiling. Flanking the chapel at a lower level are two large stone pylons upon which are maps made of various inlaid granites (see pp. 6–7). Inscriptions remember the achievements of the American armed forces in this region and the names of 371 of the missing. Rosettes mark the names of those since recovered and identified. Sloping gently downhill from the memorial is the burial area containing 5,076 of our military dead, many of whom lost their lives in the Battle of the Bulge and in the advance to the Rhine River.

Ardennes American Cemetery and Memorial

The memorial is a stone structure bearing on its façade a massive American eagle and other sculptures. Within the memorial is the chapel, three large wall maps composed of inlaid marbles, marble panels depicting combat and supply activities and other ornamental features. Along the outside of the memorial, 462 names are inscribed on the granite Tablets of the Missing. Rosettes mark the names of those since recovered and identified. The façade on the far north end, that overlooks the burial area,

Above Left and Right: *The Ardennes American Memorial and Cemetery in Neupré Belgium. The insignia clockwise from top: Supreme HQ Allied Expeditionary Forces; Comms Zone ETO; Sixth Army Group; Ninth Air Force; Ninth Army; First Army (above); Seventh Army (below); Third Army; Eighth Air Force; Twelfth Army Group; U.S. Strategic Air Forces in Europe.*

Right: *This eagle memorial commemorates the "Screaming Eagles"—the 101st Airborne Division—who were the primary defenders of the besieged city. Donated by the city of Bastogne and its inhabitants it can be found near the Mardasson Memorial and the text on the plaque reads: "May this eagle always symbolize the sacrifices and heroism of the 101st Airborne Division and all its attached units."*

bears the insignia, in mosaic, of the major U.S. units that operated in northwest Europe in World War II. The 90-acre cemetery contains the graves of 5,323 of our military dead, many of whom died during the Battle of the Bulge.

Mardasson Bastogne Memorial

The Mardasson Memorial honors the memory of 76,890 American soldiers who were wounded or killed during the Battle of the Bulge. Architect Georges Dedoyard designed the complex as a five-pointed star, the inner walls covered by descriptions of the battle. The outer crown is engraved with the names of the contemporary 48 U.S. states with Alaska and Hawaii, and the insignia of most participating battalions are shown on the walls. Below the crown, there's a crypt with three altars—one each for Protestant, Catholic and Jewish services—was carved, and decorated with mosaics by French artist Fernand Léger. The monument was dedicated on July 16, 1950. Next to it, the excellent Bastogne War Museum opened in March 2014.

Above left and Right: *The star-shaped Mardasson Memorial.*

Below: *CWGC Hotton Cemetery.* Juegopasivo/ WikiCommons (CC BY-SA 4.0)

CWGC Hotton Cemetery

There are hundreds of British cemeteries in Belgium, administered by the Commonwealth War Graves Commission, with the dead of two world wars. Hotton Cemetery contains 666 graves—most of them soldiers who died during the last fall and winter of World War II, although some are from 1940. It was from Hotton that 53rd Welsh Division, supported by tanks of the 1st Northamptonshire Yeomanry Regiment and the 144th R.A.C. Regiment, launched its attack.

Above: *Crucifixion group on the crypt in Lommel cemetery.*

Above Right and Opposite:
German war graves in Recogne near Foy. There are no Allied war cemeteries near Bastogne any more, since postwar the graves were moved further north to the Henri-Chapelle American Cemetery and Memorial near Liège. Today, the remains of over 6,800 Axis soldiers, victims of the fighting around Bastogne as well as of the previous invasion and occupation of Belgium, are buried in the German war cemetery at Recogne near Foy. The site is maintained by the German War Graves Commission and consists of a small chapel next to a field of simple stone crosses, each having up to six names inscribed.

Right: *Sandweiler cemetery in Luxembourg.*

German Cemeteries

The German War Graves Commission (*Volksbund Deutsche Kriegsgräberfürsorge*) is responsible for the maintenance and upkeep of German war graves in Europe and North Africa. The three cemeteries that hold the bulk of Battle of the Bulge dead are

*   Recogne/Foy near Bastogne in Belgium, which contains the graves of 6,807 German soldiers.
*   Lommel, in Belgium, the largest German military cemetery in Western Europe outside Germany itself. It holds dead from both world wars—38,560 from World War II and 542 from World War I.
*   Sandweiler—5,286 servicemen were moved here from 150 different cemeteries throughout Luxembourg.

Above: *Postwar, the Touring Club de Belgique erected twenty-six battlefield markers showing the greatest extent of the German advances and the Bastogne perimeter. They are all shown in Pallud's wonderful tome. The inscription reads, "Ici fut arrete l'envahisseur" (here the invader was stopped). These are at the bridge in Hotton, Stoumont station, and Stavelot.*

CREDITS & BIBLIOGRAPHY

First and foremost grateful thanks go to **Battle-fieldHistorian.com**: this book wouldn't have been possible without photos from this brilliant website. Thanks, too, to NARA, College Park, MD, and the George Forty Library for the other historic photos. Other credits are noted on the photographs. If anyone is missing or incorrectly credited, apologies! Please notify the author through the publishers.

The unit insignia are from WikiCommons, specifically: Thadius856 (Ninth Army), Willtron (LSSAH), Resigua (Das Reich, Hohenstaufen), Jecowa (Hitlerjugend), Vasyatka1(212th VGD), Joeyeti CC BY-SA 3.0 (276th VGD), RRskaReb CC BY-SA 4.0 (5th FJR), Marco Kaiser (2nd, 9th, 116th Pz), Ignasi (XXX Corps), Noclador (7th Armd).

Other thanks are due to Elly for design work; Richard Wood for ferrying me round the Ardennes and for his photographs; the military cyclists for photos and enthusiasm; Marcus Cowper at Osprey for providing background reading; and, of course, Leo Marriott for the aerial photographs and for mentorship at NARA.

The Series M404 (4072), Great Britain War Office, 1942, maps are from the online resources of the University of Texas, Perry-Castañeda Library Map Collection collection. The U.S. official maps are from the various "Green Books" which can be found online at the U.S. Army Center of Military History.

The maps on pp. 16–19 are from the Library of Congress' Geography and Map Division. Otherwise the artwork is, as usual, by Mark Franklin.

Online sources include:
http://allworldwars.com/German-Radio-Intelligence-by-Albert-Praun.html#1
https://www.med-dept.com/ Great info on all things medical.
http://ww2today.com Day-by-day coverage of the war with photos and articles; always interesting.
http://www.history.army.mil The U.S. Center of Military History is a wonderful location for the official histories and much more.
http://ibiblio.org/hyperwar/USA/SCAEF-Report/index.html Text of Report by The Supreme Commander To the Combined Chiefs of Staff On the Operations in Europe of the Allied Expeditionary Force 6 June 1944 to 8 May 1945.
http://ww2talk.com Fantastic discussion forum populated by people who know stuff.
http://www.tracesofwar.com/ Indispensible site!

Books and magazine articles
The best books to start any research on the Ardennes are undoubtedly Hugh Cole's Green Book (I used the 1993 50th anniversary version) and Jean Pallud's Then and Now treatment. There are many others!

After Action Report 90th Inf Div January–May 1945; retrieved through http://www.90thdivisionassoc.org.
After Action Report 801st TD Battalion retrieved through Ike Skelton Combined Arms Research Library Digital Library.
After the Battle: magazines and books, especially Pallud (see below).
American Battle Monuments Commission leaflets (provided much of the information about the cemeteries).
Bergstrom, Christer: The Ardennes 1944–1945; Vaktel Förlag/Casemate, 2014.
Biggio, Col Charles P.: "American and German field artillery in the Battle of the Bulge"; retrieved from Checkerboard, the 99th Division Association website. Info used in Artillery section on p. 24.
Buckley, John: Monty's Men: The British Army and the Liberation of Europe; Yale University Press, 2013.
Carter, Col William R.: "Air Power in the Battle of the Bulge: A Theater Campaign Perspective"; Airpower Journal, 1989; retrieved from http://www.airuniversity.af.mil.
Cavanagh, William C. C., and Karl: A Tour of the Bulge Battlefields; Pen & Sword, 2016.
Cole, Hugh M.: US Army in World War II The European Theater of Operations The Ardennes: Battle of the Bulge; CMH, 1965, new edition 1993.
Cooke, David, and Evans, Wayne: Kampfgruppe Peiper The Race for the Meuse; Pen & Sword, 2014.
D'Este: Patton A Genius for War; HarperCollins, 1995.
Dupuy, Trevor: Hitler's Last Gamble; HarperCollins, 1994.
ETHINT 10: "Interview With Joachim Peiper by Major Kenneth W. Hechler"; U.S. Army, 1945. Retrieved from https://www.merriam-press.com/ww2ejour/articles/iss_001/is001_06.htm
Forty, George: The Reich's Last Gamble; Cassel & Co, 2001.
Girbig, Werner: Six Months To Oblivion The Eclipse of the Luftwaffe Fighter Force; Ian Allan Ltd, 1975.
Goldstein, Donald M., Dillon, Katherine V., and Wenger, J. Michael: Nuts! The Battle of the Bulge The Story and Photographs; Prange Enterprises Inc, 1994.
Haasler Timm, MacDougall, Roddy, Vosters, Simon, and Weber, Hans: Duel in the Mist 2; Panzerwrecks, 2012.
Haasler Timm, Vosters, Simon, and Weber, Hans: Duel in the Mist 3; Panzerwrecks, 2014.
Hallion, Richard P.: The US Army Air Forces in WW2 D-Day 19 44 Air Power Over the Normandy Beaches and Beyond; Air Force History and Museums Program, 1994.
Hofmann, George F.: The Super Sixth; Sixth Armored Division Assoc, 1975.
Jarkowsky, Maj Jeffrey: German Special Operations in the 1944 Ardennes Offensive; Fort Leavenworth, Kansas 1994 (retrieved digitally).
Kays, Marvin D.: Weather Effects During the Battle of the Bulge and the Normandy Invasion; US Army Electronics Research and Development Command, 1982 (retrieved digitally). Much of the information on pp. 32–33 comes from this paper.
Kennedy, Jr., Maj James L.: The Failure of German Logistics During the Ardennes Offensive of 1944; Fort Leavenworth, KS, 2000 (retrieved digitally).
King, Martin, Collins, Michael, and Hillborn, David: The Fighting 30th Division; Casemate, 1995.
Konings, Bob: "Eric Fisher Wood"; article from http://www.battle-of-the-bulge.be/eric-fisher-wood/
Kreuder, Gregory: Lieutenant General "Pete" Quesada and Generalfeldmarschall Wolfram Von Richthofen: What Made Them Great?; thesis, June 2009 retrieved from www.dtic.mil/get-tr-doc/pdf?AD=ADA540546.
MacDonald, Charles B.: A Time for Trumpets; William Morrow, 1997.
MacDonald, Charles B.: The Battle of the Bulge; Weidenfeld Paperbacks, 1984.
Manrho, John and Putz, Ron: Bodenplatte: The Luftwaffe's Last Hope; Hikoki Publications, 2004.
Mark, Eduard: Aerial Interdiction Air Power and the Land Battle in Three American Wars; Center for Air Force History, 1994.
Milmeister, Jean: "Identifying the Clervaux Castle Sherman"; from http://www.diorama-clervaux.com/indexsherman.html
Nordyke, Phil: All American All the Way; Zenith Press, 2005.
Pamp, Capt Frederick E., Jr: From Normandy to the Elbe: XIX Corps history.
Pallud, Jean Paul: Battle of the Bulge Then and Now; After the Battle, 1984.
Patton, George S.: War As I Knew It; Houghton Mifflin, 1947.
Quarrie, Bruce: Order of Battle 4 The Ardennes Offensive Northern Sector VI Panzerarmee; Osprey, 1999.
_____: Order of Battle 5 The Ardennes Offensive Northern Sector V US Corps & XVIII US (Airborne) Corps; Osprey, 1999.
_____: Order of Battle 8 The Ardennes Offensive Central Sector V Panzerarmee; Osprey, 2000.
_____: Order of Battle 9 The Ardennes Offensive Central Sector US VII & VIII Corps and British XXX Corps; Osprey, 2000.
Reynolds, Michael: The Devil's Adjutant, Jochen Peiper Panzer Leader; Spellmount/Sarpedon, 1995.
Rutledge, William E., Jr: Combat History of the Sixth Armored Division; found on http://www.super6th.org; 1947.
Sharpe, Michael, & Davis, Brian L.: Spearhead 5 Leibstandarte; Ian Allan Ltd, 2002.
Schneider, Wolfgang: Tigers in Combat I/II; Stackpole, 2000/1998.
Stone, Thomas R.: "General William Hood Simpson: Unsung Commander of US Ninth Army"; Parameters, Journal of the US Army War College, 1981; retrieved from www.dtic.mil/get-tr-doc/pdf?AD=ADA510095
USAREUR: Battle Book The Battle of the Bulge.
Various authors: US Army in World War II The Technical Services The Corps of Engineers: The War Against Germany; US Center of Military History, 1985.
Wilbeck, Maj Christopher W.: Sledgehammers: Strengths and Flaws of Tiger Tank Battalions in World War II; The Aberjona Press, 2004.
Yeide, Harry: Fighting Patton: George S. Patton Jr. Though the Eyes of His Enemies; Zenith Press, 2011.

Opposite: Memorials at (T–B)— Vielsalm; Ourthe; a German one at Losheimergraben; and 505th PIR at Trois-Ponts.

GLOSSARY

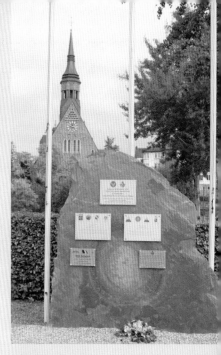

2TAF 2nd Tactical Air Force, RAF
Abt *Abteilung*
AEAF Allied Expeditionary Air Force
AIB armored infantry battalion
AP armor-piercing
armd armored (as in 2nd Armd Div)
ARV armored recovery vehicle
ATk antitank
BD Bombardment Division
Bn battalion
CCA/B/R Combat Command A/B/R
CEBA *Cercle d'études sur la Bataille des Ardennes* (Belgian study group on the Battle of the Bulge)
Coy(s) company(ies)
CP command post
CWGC Commonwealth War Graves Commission
DB *Division Blindée* = armd div
Div division
ECB Engineer Combat Bn
FA field artillery
FJR *Fallschirmjäger* = German paratrooper
FJR6 6th Regt of 2nd FJR Div
Flak *Flugzeugabwehrkanone* = AAA
GMC gun motor carriage
GR *Grenadier Regt* (German infantry)
Grp group
HMC howitzer motor carriage
ID/R infantry division/regiment

IFF Identification Friend/Foe
JG *Jagdgeschwader* = bomber wing
KG *Kampfgruppe* = battle group, ersatz combinations of troops that happened to be available at a given time. Usually named for their commander.
KO knocked out. If used about armored vehicles this didn't necessarily mean that they were destroyed. Battlefield recovery, refurbishment in battlefield workshops, and reuse in battle was frequent on both sides.
KwK *Kampfwagenkanone* = tank gun
le/sFH *leichte/schwerer Feldhaubitze* = light/heavy field howitzer
LSSAH *Leibstandarte-SS Adolf Hitler* = 1st SS-Panzer Division
m *mittlere* = medium
MEW microwave early warning
OB West *Oberbefehlshaber West* = C-in-C West
OKH/L/M/W *Oberkommando des Heeres/der Luftwaffe/der Marine/der Wehrmacht* = Army/Airforce/Navy/Armed forces High Command
PaK *Panzerabwehrkanone* = ATk gun
PIAT Projector Infantry Anti Tank
PIR parachute infantry regiment
PzGr *Panzergrenadier* = armored

infantry
Pionier military engineer
RAC Royal Armoured Corps (BR)
RAF Royal Air Force
RCT Regimental Combat Team
Recon reconnaissance (US)
recce reconnaissance (UK)
Regt regiment
RTR Royal Tank Regiment (3RTR = 3rd Royal Tank Regiment
S-mine *Schuh-mine* = anti-personnel mine
SdKfz *Sonderkraftfahrzeug* = special purpose vehicle
SG *Schlachtgeschwader* = close-support wing
SIGINT signals intelligence
(SS-) sPzAbt *(SS-)schwere Panzer-Abteilung* = (SS-) heavy tank battalion (Tiger I and II)
SPW *schwerer Panzerspähwagen* = heavy armd recon vehicle
Sqn squadron
StuG *Sturmgeschütz* = assault gun
TAC Tactical Air Command
TD tank destroyer—could mean towed ATk guns or tracked (M10, M18 or M36)
USAAF US Army Air Force
VG Division *Volksgrenadier* Division = "People's" rifle division. A late war designation, most VGDs were built around a cadre of experienced officers and NCOs. Some fought very well.

INDEX

Allied major units
air assets: 2TAF, 20; IX TAC, 20, 21, 104; XIX TAC 20, 158, 174, 179; XXIX TAC, 20
British units:
21st Army Group, 9, 12, 15, 28
Army: Second, 11
Corps: XXX, 9–11, 12, 19, 110, 142, 155, 158, 181, 190
Division: 6th Airborne, 12, 19, 69; 43rd (Wessex) Inf, 12, 19; 50th (Northumbrian), 19; 51st Highland, 11, 12, 19, 158; 53rd (Welsh) Inf, 12, 19, 158, 187; Guards Armoured, 12, 19
Armd Bde: 29th, 10, 12, 19, 112, 155; 33rd, 12, 19, 158
Regiments: 2nd Fife and Forfar Yeomanry, 19, 153; 23rd Hussars, 19; 3RTR, 19, 139, 142, 152, 155
U.S. Units:
Army Group: 12th, 8, 9, 11, 12, 68
Army: First, 8–11, 12, 13, 15, 19, 20, 54, 68, 69, 72, 74, 107, 110, 131, 142, 168, 169, 176,

181, 186; Third, 8–11, 12, 13, 14, 15, 18, 20, 62, 68, 69, 72, 80, 131, 132, 136, 137, 138, 139, 152, 158, 169, 169, 174, 181, 185, 186; Seventh, 11, 14, 139, 184, 186, 190; Ninth, 11, 12, 15, 68, 74, 110, 139, 184, 186, 190
Corps: III, 10, 12, 14, 68, 132, 142, 162; V, 12, 13, 24, 45, 119; VI, 11; VII Corps, 11, 12, 110, 142, 150, 152, 176; VIII, 10, 11, 12, 13, 68, 115, 132, 142; XII, 12, 132; XIII, 12, 13, 15; XVI, 12; XVIII Airborne, 12, 50, 91, 110, 142, 176; XIX, 12, 15; XX, 14
Division: 1st Inf, 12, 13, 35, 43, 44, 45, 68; 2nd Armd, 10, 12, 19, 24, 30, 83, 115, 131, 139, 142, 166; 2nd Inf, 12, 13, 17, 24, 35, 41, 42, 44, 45, 50, 53, 101; 3rd Armd Div, 12, 33, 54, 70, 85, 87, 105, 107, 110, 142, 143, 147, 149, 150, 151, 170, 172, 176; 4th Armd Div, 10, 12, 14, 68, 69, 72, 131, 132, 134, 137, 138, 163; 4th Inf, 12,

13, 58, 60, 65, 134; 5th Armd Div, 12, 62, 160; 5th Inf, 12, 62, 65, 173, 181; 6th Armd Div, 4, 12, 127, 160, 162–165; 7th Armd Div, 2, 12, 15, 25, 50, 54, 68, 98, 100, 105, 110, 166, 170, 176, 190; 8th Inf, 12; 9th Armd Div, 12, 13, 49, 50, 53, 58, 62, 63, 72, 83, 110, 114, 115, 116, 176; 9th Inf, 12; 10th Armd Div, 12, 50, 58, 60, 65, 68, 69, 72, 114, 115, 116, 118, 119, 120, 121, 122, 132, 162, 163, 176; 11th Armd Div, 11, 12, 124, 158, 160, 168, 169; 17th AB, 12, 65; 26th Inf, 12, 26, 65; 28th Inf, 12, 13, 17, 50, 53, 57, 58, 60, 62, 63, 65, 69, 100, 114, 115, 116, 150, 163, 176; 29th Inf, 12; 30th Inf, 12, 13, 15, 24, 36, 68, 74–75, 85, 86, 88, 105; 35th Inf, 2, 12, 161; 75th Inf, 12, 110, 149, 153; 78th Inf, 12; 80th Inf, 12, 62, 65, 69, 172, 179; 82nd AB, 9, 12, 24, 35, 68, 70–71, 72, 73, 85, 90, 91, 102, 105, 110,